CONTENTS

CHAPTER 1 • Numbers 1 to 10

Mixed Review 1

One, Two, Three 2

Four and Five 3

Zero 4

Numbers to 10 5

Six, Seven, Eight 6

Nine and Ten 7

Problem-Solving Strategy: Use a Pattern 8

Order Numbers 9

Count Pennies 10

Problem Solving: Number Patterns 11

CHAPTER 2 • Exploring Part–Part–Whole

Mixed Review 12

Make Cube Trains 13

Parts and Totals 14

Problem-Solving Strategy: Act It Out 15

More Parts and Totals 16

Find the Total 17

Mixed Review 18

Find the Missing Part 19

Problem Solving: What Is the Question? 20

CHAPTER 3 • Beginning to Add

Mixed Review 21

Addition Sentences 22

More Addition Sentences 23

Problem-Solving Strategy: Write an Addition Sentence 24

Addition Fact Pairs 25

Counting On 26

More Counting On 27

Problem Solving: Can You Add to Solve? 28

CHAPTER 4 • Beginning to Subtract

Mixed Review 29

Subtraction Sentences 30

More Subtraction Sentences 31

Problem-Solving Strategy: Write a Subtraction Sentence . . . 32

Subtraction Fact Pairs 33

Counting Back 34

More Counting Back 35

Problem Solving: Can You Subtract to Solve? 36

CHAPTER 5 • Adding and Subtracting to 10

Mixed Review 37

Vertical Addition 38

Related Addition Facts 39

Add Money 40

Mixed Review 41

Vertical Subtraction 42

Related Subtraction Facts 43

Subtract Money 44

Addition and Subtraction 45

Problem-Solving Strategy: Choose the Operation 46

Problem Solving: Use a Picture 47

CHAPTER 6 • Numbers to 100 and Graphing

Mixed Review 48

Numbers to 20 49

Count to 50 50

Numbers to 50 51

Problem-Solving Strategy: Use Estimation 52

Count to 100 53

Numbers to 100 54

Order to 100 55

Before, After, Between 56

Skip-Count 57

More Skip-Counting 58

Greater and Less 59

Ordinal Numbers 60

Mixed Review 61

Bar Graphs 62

Problem Solving: Use a Graph 63

CHAPTER 7 • Geometry and Fractions

Mixed Review 64

2- and 3-Dimensional Shapes 65

2-Dimensional Shapes 66

Problem-Solving Strategy: Use a Physical Model 67

Mixed Review 68

Halves 69

Fourths 70

Thirds 71

Problem Solving: Draw a Picture 72

CHAPTER 8 • Money

Pennies and Nickels 73

Pennies and Dimes 74

Mixed Review 75

More Counting Money 76

Problem-Solving Strategy: Guess and Test 77

Quarters 78

Mixed Review 79

More Comparing Money 80

Problem Solving: Use Data from a Table 81

CHAPTER 9 • Time

Mixed Review 82

Hour 83

Time to the Hour 84

Half Hour 85

Time to the Half Hour 86

Problem-Solving Strategy: Make a List 87

Mixed Review 88

More About Calendars 89

Problem Solving: Use Estimation 90

CHAPTER 10 • Adding and Subtracting to 18

Doubles 91

Doubles Plus 1 92

Mixed Review 93

Add 94

Add Three Numbers 95

Mixed Review 96

Subtract 97

More Subtracting 98

Problem-Solving Strategy: Choose the Operation 99

Add and Subtract 100

Fact Families 101

Problem Solving: Choose a Strategy 102

CHAPTER 11 • Exploring Measurement

Mixed Review 103

Measure Length 104

Inch 105

Foot 106

Centimeter 107

Problem-Solving Strategy: Draw a Picture 108

Pound 109

Cup 110

Mixed Review 111

Problem Solving: Choose Reasonable Numbers 112

CHAPTER 12 • Exploring 2-Digit Addition and Subtraction

Mixed Review 113

Add Facts and Tens 114

Count On by Tens 115

2-Digit Addition 116

More Addition 117

Problem-Solving Strategy: Use Estimation 118

Mixed Review 119

Subtract Facts and Tens 120

Count Back by Tens 121

2-Digit Subtraction 122

More Subtraction 123

Problem Solving: Choose the Method 124

MIXED REVIEW

Match.

ONE, TWO, THREE

Count.	Draw.	Write.

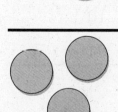

FOUR AND FIVE

Count.	Draw.	Write.

Grade 1, Chapter 1, Lesson 2, Day 2, pages 9–10

Name:

ZERO

Count. Write how many.

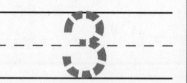

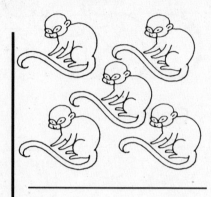

NUMBERS TO 10

Count. Draw a set with fewer.

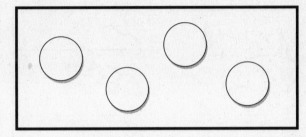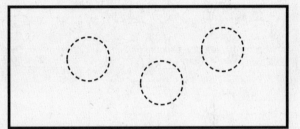

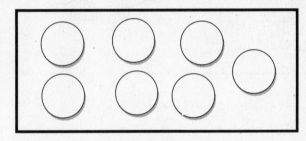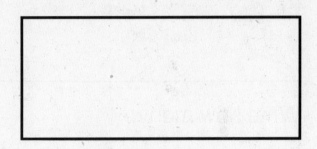

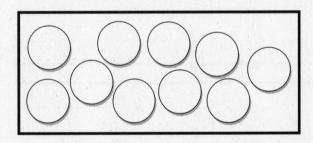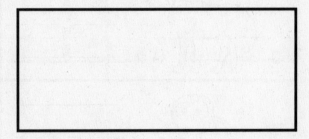

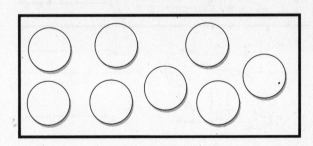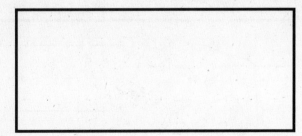

SIX, SEVEN, EIGHT

Write how many.

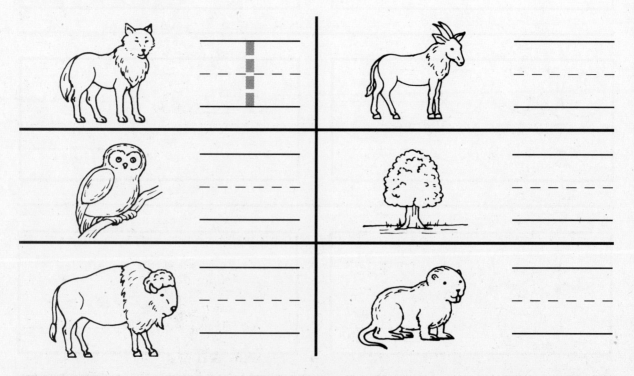

NINE AND TEN

Write how many.

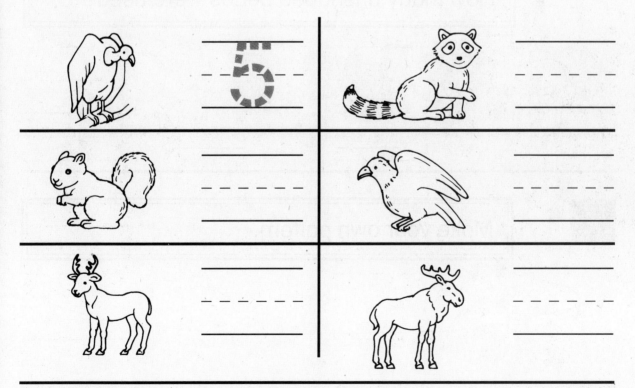

PROBLEM-SOLVING STRATEGY: USE A PATTERN

Color to show which beads come next.
How many shaded beads were used?
How many unshaded beads were used?

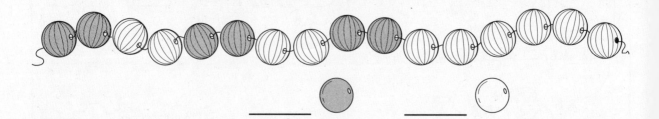

_____ 🔵   _____ ⚪

Color to show which beads come next.
How many shaded beads were used?
How many unshaded beads were used?

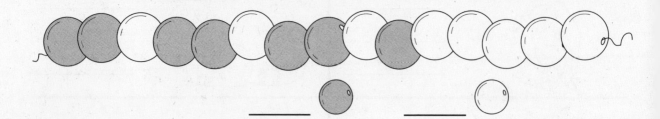

_____ 🔵   _____ ⚪

Make your own pattern.

ORDER NUMBERS

Write the numbers in order.

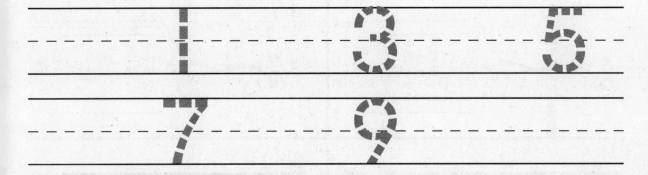

Connect the dots in order.

5.
6.
2.
1.
0.
4.
3.
7.
8.
9.
10.

COUNT PENNIES

Write how many cents.

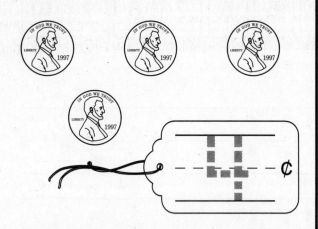

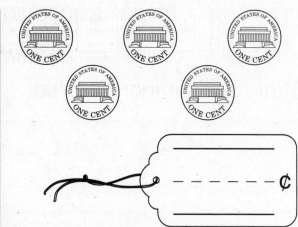

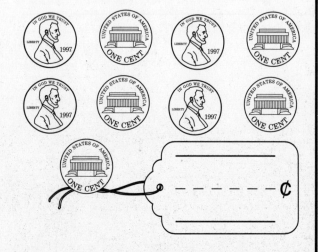

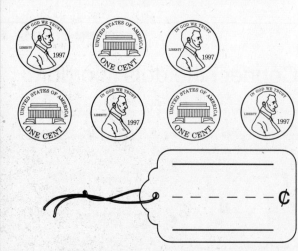

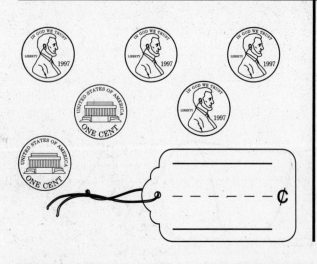

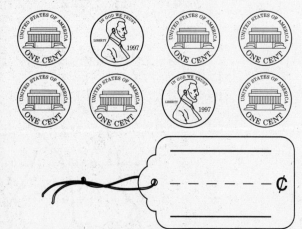

PROBLEM SOLVING: NUMBER PATTERNS

✔ Read
✔ Plan
✔ Solve
✔ Look Back

Use numbers to show the pattern.

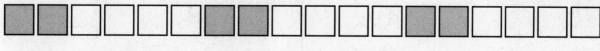

2 4 2 4 ____ ____ ____ ____

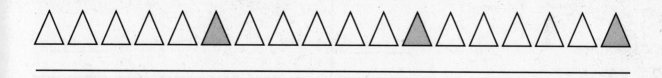

_____

- - - - - - - - - - - - - - - - - - -

_____

_____

- - - - - - - - - - - - - - - - - - -

_____

Draw a pattern.
Your partner writes the numbers.

MIXED REVIEW

Write how many.

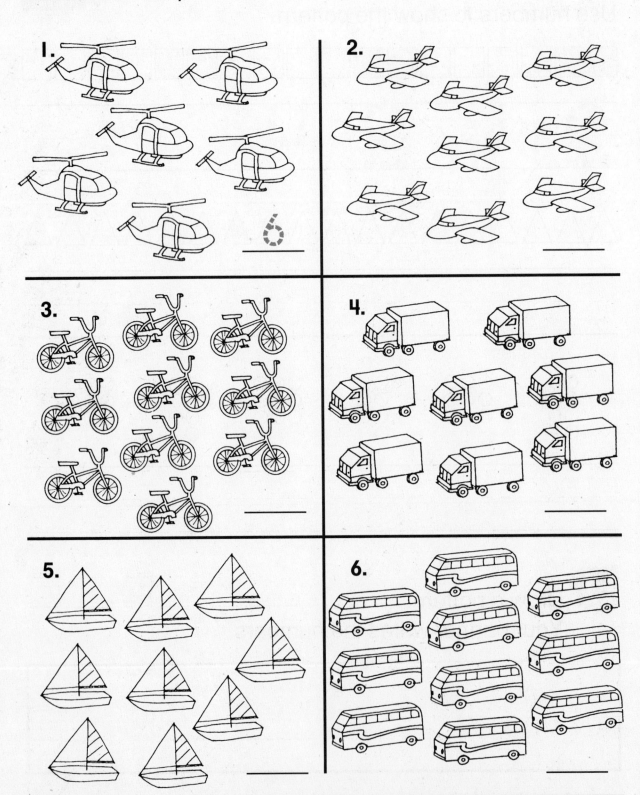

1. _____ 6

2. _____

3. _____

4. _____

5. _____

6. _____

MAKE CUBE TRAINS

Make a train for the total.
Use  and .
Draw your train.
Write how many.

Total   **Parts**

1. ⟨3⟩ _____

2. ⟨6⟩ _____ ___ ___

3. ⟨4⟩ _____ ___ ___

4. ⟨8⟩ _____ ___ ___

5. ⟨10⟩ _____ ___ ___

PARTS AND TOTALS

Make different trains for 5 with  and .
Color. Write how many.

		Parts		**Total**

1.    5   0   5

2. 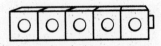   ___ ___ ___

3. 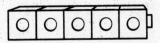   ___ ___ ___

4. 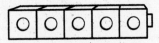   ___ ___ ___

5. 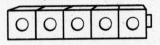   ___ ___ ___

6. 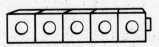   ___ ___ ___

PROBLEM-SOLVING STRATEGY: ACT IT OUT

✔ Read
✔ Plan
✔ Solve
✔ Look Back

1. At the

There are 3 grown-ups at the train station.
There are 2 children.
How many people are at the train station?

 grown-ups   children   people

2. At the

There are 5 taxis at the gas station.
There are 3 station wagons.
How many cars are at the gas station?

_____ taxis   _____ station wagons   _____ cars

3. At the

9 children are at the pool.
3 of the children are girls.
How many of the children are boys?

_____ children   _____ girls   _____ boys

MORE PARTS AND TOTALS

How many flowers in all?
Find the total.

Use ⬤ ◯ and
▦ if you want.

1.

Total: ___6___

2.

Total: _____

3.

Total: _____

4.

Total: _____

5.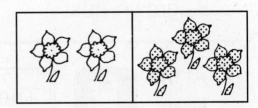

Total: _____

6.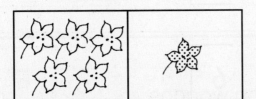

Total: _____

7.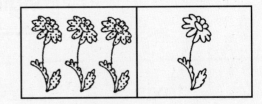

Total: _____

8.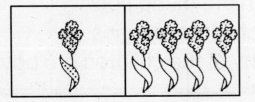

Total: _____

FIND THE TOTAL

Find the total.

Use ◐ and ▦ if you want.

1.

3	2
5	

2.

4	0

3.

3	1

4.

5	3

5.

1	2

6.

6	2

7.

4	2

8.

3	6

9.

2	8

10.

3	4

11.

0	7

12.

9	1

MIXED REVIEW

Write the missing number.

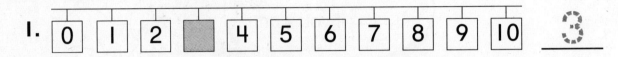

1. | 0 | 1 | 2 | ▨ | 4 | 5 | 6 | 7 | 8 | 9 | 10 | 3 ___

2. | 0 | 1 | 2 | 3 | 4 | 5 | 6 | ▨ | 8 | 9 | 10 | ___

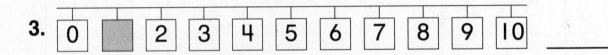

3. | 0 | ▨ | 2 | 3 | 4 | 5 | 6 | 7 | 8 | 9 | 10 | ___

Write the numbers in order.

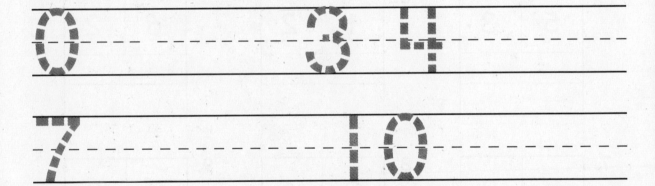

Count backward and write the numbers.

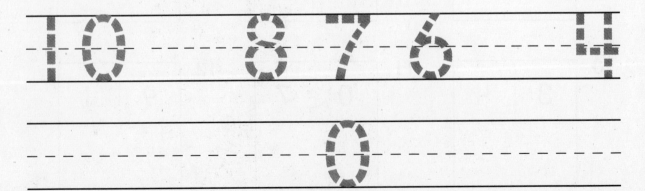

Name: _____

FIND THE MISSING PART

Find the missing part.

Use  and if you want.

1.
3	4
7	

2.
2	
5	

3.
	2
6	

4.
	5
8	

5.
6	
6	

6.
2	
8	

7.
4	
9	

8.
	6
10	

9.
	0
8	

PROBLEM SOLVING: WHAT IS THE QUESTION?

✔	Read
✔	Plan
✔	Solve
✔	Look Back

1.

Listen

There are 8 pigs on a farm.
5 are playing and the rest are sleeping.
How many pigs are sleeping?

How many are sleeping?

_8_ pigs   _5_ pigs playing   ____ pigs sleeping

2.

Listen

There are 6 cows.
2 cows have spots and the rest are black.
How many cows are black?

How many cows are black?

____ cows   ____ cows with spots   ____ black cows

MIXED REVIEW

How many in all?
Write the total.

I.   Part   Part

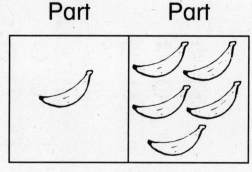

Total: _6___

2.   Part   Part

Total: ____

3.   Part   Part

Total: ____

4.   Part   Part

Total: ____

5.   Part   Part

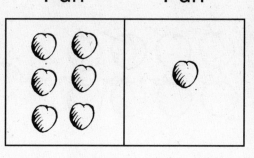

Total: ____

6.   Part   Part

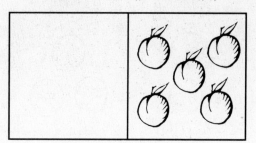

Total: ____

ADDITION SENTENCES

Add.

1.

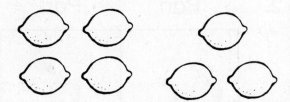

$4 + 3 = \underline{7}$

2.

$6 + 4 = \underline{}$

3.

$2 + 5 = \underline{}$

4.

$4 + 2 = \underline{}$

5.

$2 + 3 = \underline{}$

6.

$8 + 1 = \underline{}$

MORE ADDITION SENTENCES

Write the addition sentences.

1.

__4__ + __2__ = __6__

2.

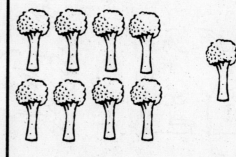

___ + ___ = ___

3.

___ + ___ = ___

4.

___ + ___ = ___

5.

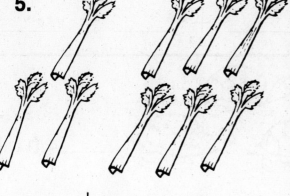

___ + ___ = ___

6.

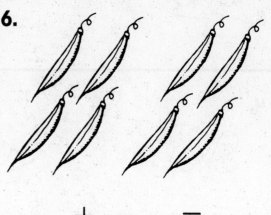

___ + ___ = ___

PROBLEM-SOLVING STRATEGY: WRITE AN ADDITION SENTENCE

✔	Read
✔	Plan
✔	Solve
✔	Look Back

Find how many in all.
Write the addition sentence.

1.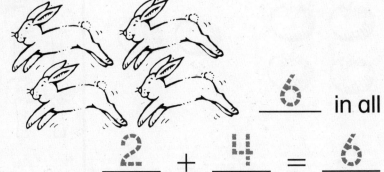

____6____ in all

__2__ + __4__ = __6__

2.

_____ in all

____ + ____ = ____

3.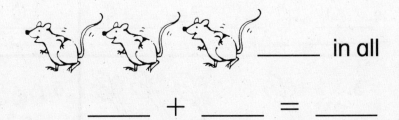

_____ in all

____ + ____ = ____

4.

_____ in all

____ + ____ = ____

ADDITION FACT PAIRS

Add.

1.

Use if you want.

$$2¢ \; + \; 6¢ \; = \; \underline{8}¢$$

2.
$$3¢ + 5¢ = \underline{\quad}¢$$
$$5¢ + 3¢ = \underline{\quad}¢$$

3.
$$6¢ + 4¢ = \underline{\quad}¢$$
$$4¢ + 6¢ = \underline{\quad}¢$$

4.
$$0¢ + 6¢ = \underline{\quad}¢$$
$$6¢ + 0¢ = \underline{\quad}¢$$

5.
$$3¢ + 1¢ = \underline{\quad}¢$$
$$1¢ + 3¢ = \underline{\quad}¢$$

6.
$$5¢ + 1¢ = \underline{\quad}¢$$
$$1¢ + 5¢ = \underline{\quad}¢$$

7.
$$0¢ + 8¢ = \underline{\quad}¢$$
$$8¢ + 0¢ = \underline{\quad}¢$$

8.
$$3¢ + 6¢ = \underline{\quad}¢$$
$$6¢ + 3¢ = \underline{\quad}¢$$

9.
$$0¢ + 7¢ = \underline{\quad}¢$$
$$7¢ + 0¢ = \underline{\quad}¢$$

COUNTING ON

Count on to add.

1.

$7 + 1 = \underline{8}$

2.

$5 + 3 = \underline{8}$

Add. Then color.

4	5 or 6	7 or 8	9 or 10
yellow	orange	brown	red

$6 + 3 = \underline{}$

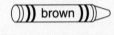
$2 + 2 = \underline{}$

$4 + 1 = \underline{}$

$3 + 2 = \underline{}$

$7 + 2 = \underline{}$

$5 + 1 = \underline{}$

$8 + 2 = \underline{}$

$4 + 3 = \underline{}$

$6 + 2 = \underline{}$

$5 + 2 = \underline{}$

MORE COUNTING ON

Add.
Use a number line to count on.

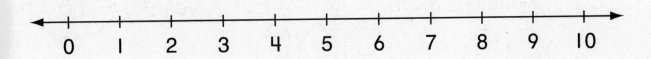

0 1 2 3 4 5 6 7 8 9 10

Color sums 4 and 5 (yellow). Color sums 6 and 7 (green).
Color sums 8 and 9 (purple). Color sum 10 (red).

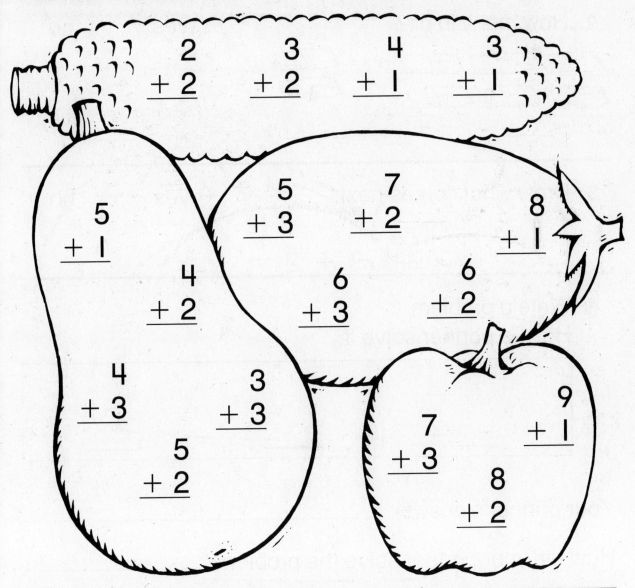

$$\begin{array}{c} 2 \\ +2 \end{array} \quad \begin{array}{c} 3 \\ +2 \end{array} \quad \begin{array}{c} 4 \\ +1 \end{array} \quad \begin{array}{c} 3 \\ +1 \end{array}$$

$$\begin{array}{c} 5 \\ +1 \end{array} \quad \begin{array}{c} 5 \\ +3 \end{array} \quad \begin{array}{c} 7 \\ +2 \end{array} \quad \begin{array}{c} 8 \\ +1 \end{array}$$

$$\begin{array}{c} 4 \\ +2 \end{array} \quad \begin{array}{c} 6 \\ +3 \end{array} \quad \begin{array}{c} 6 \\ +2 \end{array}$$

$$\begin{array}{c} 4 \\ +3 \end{array} \quad \begin{array}{c} 3 \\ +3 \end{array}$$

$$\begin{array}{c} 5 \\ +2 \end{array} \quad \begin{array}{c} 7 \\ +3 \end{array} \quad \begin{array}{c} 9 \\ +1 \end{array}$$

$$\begin{array}{c} 8 \\ +2 \end{array}$$

PROBLEM SOLVING: CAN YOU ADD TO SOLVE?

Solve. Ring **yes** or **no**.

Can you add?

1. Ring which is more.

yes no

3

4

2. How many in all?

yes   no

___ + ___ = ___

3. Draw what comes next.

yes   no

4. Write a problem.
   Have a partner solve it.

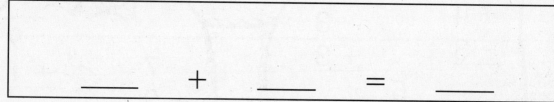

___ + ___ = ___

Your partner's answer _____

How did your partner solve the problem? _____

Name: _____

MIXED REVIEW

Write the addition sentence.

1.

$\underline{3} + \underline{4} = \underline{7}$

2.

___ + ___ = ___

3.

___ + ___ = ___

4.

___ + ___ = ___

Count on to add.

5.
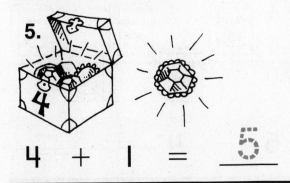

$4 + 1 = \underline{5}$

6.
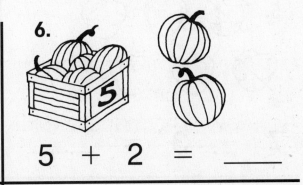

$5 + 2 = \underline{}$

7.

$7 + 2 = \underline{}$

8.
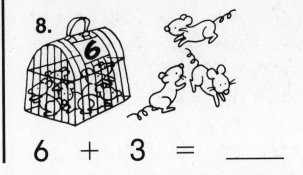

$6 + 3 = \underline{}$

SUBTRACTION SENTENCES

Find what is left.

1.

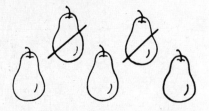

5 − 2 = _**3**_

2.

3 − 1 = ____

3.

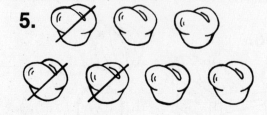

9 − 7 = ____

4.

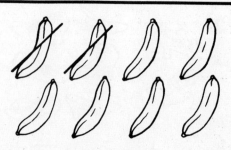

8 − 2 = ____

5.

7 − 3 = ____

6.

5 − 4 = ____

7.

9 − 6 = ____

8.

6 − 4 = ____

MORE SUBTRACTION SENTENCES

Write the subtraction sentence.

1.

$3 - 2 = 1$

2.

___ − ___ = ___

3.

___ − ___ = ___

4.

___ − ___ = ___

5.

___ − ___ = ___

6.
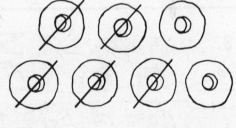

___ − ___ = ___

7.

___ − ___ = ___

8.
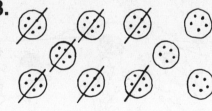

___ − ___ = ___

PROBLEM-SOLVING STRATEGY: WRITE A SUBTRACTION SENTENCE

Find how many are left.
Write the subtraction sentence.

1.

_3_ are left.

_5_ – _2_ = _3_

2.

____ are left.

____ – ____ = ____

3.

____ are left.

____ – ____ = ____

4.

____ are left.

____ – ____ = ____

SUBTRACTION FACT PAIRS

Subtract.

1.

$$6¢ - 5¢ = \underline{\hspace{1cm}}¢$$

2.
$$3¢ - 2¢ = \underline{\hspace{1cm}}¢$$
$$3¢ - 1¢ = \underline{\hspace{1cm}}¢$$

3.
$$5¢ - 0¢ = \underline{\hspace{1cm}}¢$$
$$5¢ - 5¢ = \underline{\hspace{1cm}}¢$$

4.
$$9¢ - 7¢ = \underline{\hspace{1cm}}¢$$
$$9¢ - 2¢ = \underline{\hspace{1cm}}¢$$

5.
$$7¢ - 4¢ = \underline{\hspace{1cm}}¢$$
$$7¢ - 3¢ = \underline{\hspace{1cm}}¢$$

6.
$$8¢ - 7¢ = \underline{\hspace{1cm}}¢$$
$$8¢ - 1¢ = \underline{\hspace{1cm}}¢$$

7.
$$4¢ - 3¢ = \underline{\hspace{1cm}}¢$$
$$4¢ - 1¢ = \underline{\hspace{1cm}}¢$$

8.
$$9¢ - 3¢ = \underline{\hspace{1cm}}¢$$
$$9¢ - 6¢ = \underline{\hspace{1cm}}¢$$

9.
$$8¢ - 6¢ = \underline{\hspace{1cm}}¢$$
$$8¢ - 2¢ = \underline{\hspace{1cm}}¢$$

COUNTING BACK

Count back to subtract.

1.

4 − 1 = _3_

2. 3 − 2 = ____   3. 8 − 2 = ____

4. 9 − 1 = ____   5. 4 − 3 = ____

6. 6 − 2 = ____   7. 5 − 1 = ____

8. 5 − 2 = ____   9. 9 − 2 = ____

10. 6 − 1 = ____   11. 4 − 2 = ____

Look for a pattern. Complete.

12. 10 − 3 = ____   13. 7 − 3 = ____

    9 − 3 = ____   6 − 3 = ____

    8 − 3 = ____   5 − 3 = ____

Name: _____

MORE COUNTING BACK

Use the number line to count back to subtract.

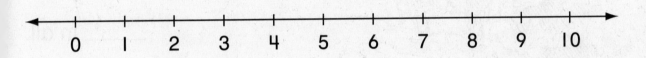

$$0 \quad 1 \quad 2 \quad 3 \quad 4 \quad 5 \quad 6 \quad 7 \quad 8 \quad 9 \quad 10$$

Count back to subtract.

1. $3 - 1 = \underline{2}$	$5 - 3 = \underline{}$	$7 - 3 = \underline{}$
2. $8 - 2 = \underline{}$	$8 - 3 = \underline{}$	$7 - 2 = \underline{}$
3. $3 - 2 = \underline{}$	$1 - 1 = \underline{}$	$4 - 3 = \underline{}$
4. $6 - 3 = \underline{}$	$5 - 1 = \underline{}$	$4 - 1 = \underline{}$
5. $8 - 1 = \underline{}$	$4 - 2 = \underline{}$	$2 - 2 = \underline{}$
6. $10 - 2 = \underline{}$	$6 - 1 = \underline{}$	$9 - 2 = \underline{}$

PROBLEM SOLVING: CAN YOU SUBTRACT TO SOLVE?

✔	Read
✔	Plan
✔	Solve
✔	Look Back

1. Listen

There were 5 deer at the lake.
2 more deer came to join them.
How many deer in all are at
the lake?

_____ in all.

_____

2. Listen

2 deer go for a walk.
How many deer are left at
the lake?

_____ are left.

_____

3. Write

Write a problem.
Have a partner solve it.

Your partner's answer _____

MIXED REVIEW

Add.

1.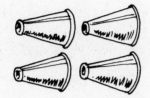

1 + 4 =

2.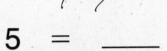

3 + 5 = ____

3.

7 + 2 = ____

4.

2 + 6 = ____

5.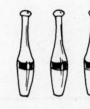

3 + 3 = ____

6.

2 + 3 = ____

7.

6 + 1 = ____

8.

4 + 3 = ____

VERTICAL ADDITION

Add.

1.

$$\begin{array}{r} 7 \\ + 2 \\ \hline 9 \end{array}$$

2.

$$\begin{array}{r} 4 \\ + 2 \\ \hline \end{array}$$

3.

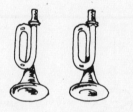

$$\begin{array}{r} 1 \\ + 2 \\ \hline \end{array}$$

4.

$$\begin{array}{r} 9 \\ + 1 \\ \hline \end{array}$$

5.

$$\begin{array}{r} 3 \\ + 2 \\ \hline \end{array}$$

6.

$$\begin{array}{r} 5 \\ + 3 \\ \hline \end{array}$$

RELATED ADDITION FACTS

Add.

1.

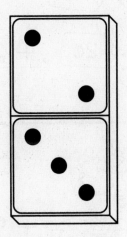

$$\begin{array}{r} 2 \\ +3 \\ \hline 5 \end{array}$$

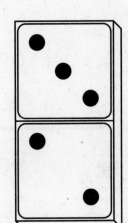

$$\begin{array}{r} 3 \\ +2 \\ \hline \end{array}$$

2.
$$\begin{array}{r} 4 \\ +2 \\ \hline \end{array} \qquad \begin{array}{r} 2 \\ +4 \\ \hline \end{array}$$
$$\begin{array}{r} 2 \\ +5 \\ \hline \end{array} \qquad \begin{array}{r} 5 \\ +2 \\ \hline \end{array}$$
$$\begin{array}{r} 1 \\ +9 \\ \hline \end{array} \qquad \begin{array}{r} 9 \\ +1 \\ \hline \end{array}$$

3.
$$\begin{array}{r} 3 \\ +5 \\ \hline \end{array} \qquad \begin{array}{r} 5 \\ +3 \\ \hline \end{array}$$
$$\begin{array}{r} 0 \\ +7 \\ \hline \end{array} \qquad \begin{array}{r} 7 \\ +0 \\ \hline \end{array}$$
$$\begin{array}{r} 6 \\ +2 \\ \hline \end{array} \qquad \begin{array}{r} 2 \\ +6 \\ \hline \end{array}$$

4.
$$\begin{array}{r} 5 \\ +4 \\ \hline \end{array} \qquad \begin{array}{r} 4 \\ +5 \\ \hline \end{array}$$
$$\begin{array}{r} 1 \\ +2 \\ \hline \end{array} \qquad \begin{array}{r} 2 \\ +1 \\ \hline \end{array}$$
$$\begin{array}{r} 2 \\ +3 \\ \hline \end{array} \qquad \begin{array}{r} 3 \\ +2 \\ \hline \end{array}$$

ADD MONEY

Add.

1. 3¢
    + 6¢
    9¢

2. 4¢
    + 2¢

3. 4¢
    + 5¢

4. 1¢
    + 9¢

5. 7¢   6¢   5¢   1¢   4¢   4¢
    + 1¢   + 4¢   + 2¢   + 7¢   + 1¢   + 3¢

6. 3¢   2¢   3¢   2¢   2¢   1¢
    + 2¢   + 7¢   + 3¢   + 8¢   + 1¢   + 6¢

7. 2¢   2¢   2¢   1¢   1¢   6¢
    + 3¢   + 2¢   + 6¢   + 5¢   + 1¢   + 3¢

MIXED REVIEW

Find what is left.

1.

$3 - 1 = \underline{2}$

2.

$5 - 2 = \underline{\hphantom{xx}}$

3.

$6 - 4 = \underline{\hphantom{xx}}$

4.

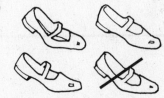

$4 - 1 = \underline{\hphantom{xx}}$

5.

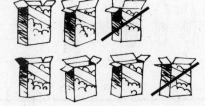

$7 - 2 = \underline{\hphantom{xx}}$

6.

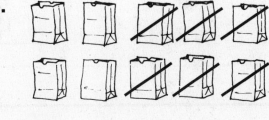

$10 - 6 = \underline{\hphantom{xx}}$

7.

$8 - 2 = \underline{\hphantom{xx}}$

8.

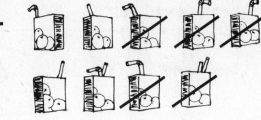

$9 - 5 = \underline{\hphantom{xx}}$

VERTICAL SUBTRACTION

Subtract.

1.

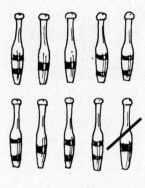

$$\begin{array}{r} 10 \\ -\ 1 \\ \hline 9 \end{array}$$

2.

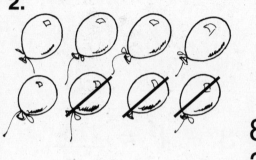

$$\begin{array}{r} 8 \\ -\ 3 \\ \hline \end{array}$$

3.

$$\begin{array}{r} 7 \\ -\ 4 \\ \hline \end{array}$$

4.

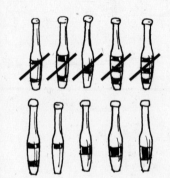

$$\begin{array}{r} 10 \\ -\ 5 \\ \hline \end{array}$$

5.

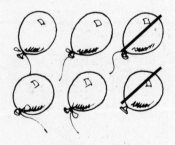

$$\begin{array}{r} 6 \\ -\ 2 \\ \hline \end{array}$$

6.

$$\begin{array}{r} 9 \\ -\ 6 \\ \hline \end{array}$$

RELATED SUBTRACTION FACTS

Subtract.

1.

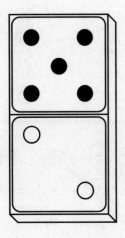
$$\begin{array}{r} 7 \\ -2 \\ \hline 5 \end{array}$$

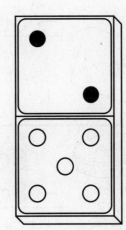
$$\begin{array}{r} 7 \\ -5 \\ \hline \end{array}$$

2.
$$\begin{array}{r} 5 \\ -3 \\ \hline \end{array} \quad \begin{array}{r} 5 \\ -2 \\ \hline \end{array}$$
$$\begin{array}{r} 4 \\ -1 \\ \hline \end{array} \quad \begin{array}{r} 4 \\ -3 \\ \hline \end{array}$$
$$\begin{array}{r} 9 \\ -2 \\ \hline \end{array} \quad \begin{array}{r} 9 \\ -7 \\ \hline \end{array}$$

3.
$$\begin{array}{r} 8 \\ -1 \\ \hline \end{array} \quad \begin{array}{r} 8 \\ -7 \\ \hline \end{array}$$
$$\begin{array}{r} 6 \\ -0 \\ \hline \end{array} \quad \begin{array}{r} 6 \\ -6 \\ \hline \end{array}$$
$$\begin{array}{r} 10 \\ -4 \\ \hline \end{array} \quad \begin{array}{r} 10 \\ -6 \\ \hline \end{array}$$

4.
$$\begin{array}{r} 9 \\ -3 \\ \hline \end{array} \quad \begin{array}{r} 9 \\ -6 \\ \hline \end{array}$$
$$\begin{array}{r} 9 \\ -4 \\ \hline \end{array} \quad \begin{array}{r} 9 \\ -5 \\ \hline \end{array}$$
$$\begin{array}{r} 5 \\ -4 \\ \hline \end{array} \quad \begin{array}{r} 5 \\ -1 \\ \hline \end{array}$$

SUBTRACT MONEY

Subtract.

1.

$$
\begin{array}{r}
10¢ \\
-\ 3¢ \\
\hline
7¢
\end{array}
$$

2.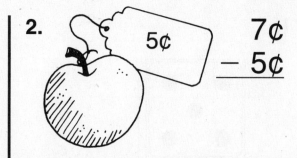

$$
\begin{array}{r}
7¢ \\
-\ 5¢ \\
\hline
\end{array}
$$

3.

$$
\begin{array}{r}
8¢ \\
-\ 8¢ \\
\hline
\end{array}
$$

4.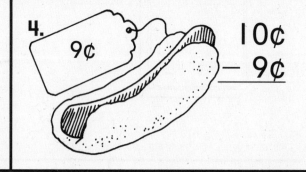

$$
\begin{array}{r}
10¢ \\
-\ 9¢ \\
\hline
\end{array}
$$

5.

$\begin{array}{r}8¢\\-\ 4¢\\\hline\end{array}$	$\begin{array}{r}9¢\\-\ 4¢\\\hline\end{array}$	$\begin{array}{r}4¢\\-\ 3¢\\\hline\end{array}$	$\begin{array}{r}3¢\\-\ 3¢\\\hline\end{array}$	$\begin{array}{r}9¢\\-\ 3¢\\\hline\end{array}$	$\begin{array}{r}10¢\\-\ 1¢\\\hline\end{array}$

6.

$\begin{array}{r}6¢\\-\ 6¢\\\hline\end{array}$	$\begin{array}{r}6¢\\-\ 4¢\\\hline\end{array}$	$\begin{array}{r}10¢\\-\ 2¢\\\hline\end{array}$	$\begin{array}{r}9¢\\-\ 7¢\\\hline\end{array}$	$\begin{array}{r}8¢\\-\ 1¢\\\hline\end{array}$	$\begin{array}{r}7¢\\-\ 5¢\\\hline\end{array}$

7.

$\begin{array}{r}9¢\\-\ 1¢\\\hline\end{array}$	$\begin{array}{r}10¢\\-\ 5¢\\\hline\end{array}$	$\begin{array}{r}8¢\\-\ 7¢\\\hline\end{array}$	$\begin{array}{r}4¢\\-\ 2¢\\\hline\end{array}$	$\begin{array}{r}5¢\\-\ 5¢\\\hline\end{array}$	$\begin{array}{r}6¢\\-\ 2¢\\\hline\end{array}$

ADDITION AND SUBTRACTION

Add or subtract.

1.
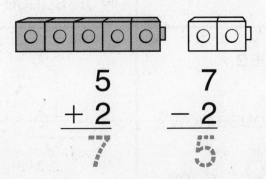

$$5 + 2 = 7$$ $$7 - 2 = 5$$

2.
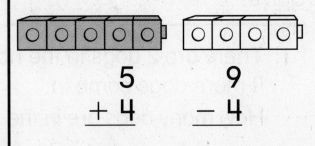

$$5 + 4$$ $$9 - 4$$

3.
$$6 + 1$$ $$7 - 1$$ $$6 + 4$$ $$10 - 4$$ $$1 + 7$$ $$8 - 7$$

4.
$$4 + 4$$ $$8 - 4$$ $$7 + 3$$ $$10 - 3$$ $$4 + 6$$ $$10 - 6$$

5.
$$2 + 8$$ $$10 - 8$$ $$1 + 0$$ $$1 - 0$$ $$4 + 5$$ $$9 - 5$$

6.
$$7 + 0$$ $$7 - 0$$ $$6 + 3$$ $$9 - 3$$ $$2 + 3$$ $$5 - 3$$

PROBLEM-SOLVING STRAGEGY: CHOOSE THE OPERATION

✔ Read
✔ Plan
✔ Solve
✔ Look Back

Choose + or −.
Solve.

	Workspace

1. There are 2 dogs in the house.
4 more dogs come in.
How many dogs are in the house now?

$\left(+\right)$ −   dogs

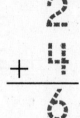

2. 6 cats are sitting.
2 cats walk away.
How many cats are still sitting?

+   −   _____ cats

3. There are 7 ducks walking.
2 more ducks join them.
How many ducks are walking now?

+   −   _____ ducks

4. 9 birds are sitting.
3 birds fly away.
How many birds are still sitting?

+   −   _____ birds

PROBLEM SOLVING: USE A PICTURE

Solve.	Workspace
1. Lana has 10¢. She buys a . How much money does she have left? _____ ¢	$\begin{array}{r} 10¢ \\ -\ 9¢ \\ \hline 1¢ \end{array}$
2. Marcus has 10¢. He buys a  . How much money does he have left? _____ ¢	
3. Sally bought a 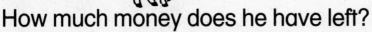 and a 🐘 . How much money did she spend? _____ ¢	

MIXED REVIEW

Add.

1.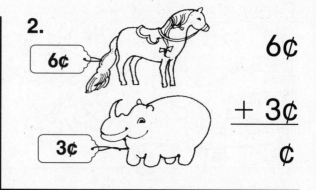

4¢
+ 5¢
9¢

2.

6¢
+ 3¢
___ ¢

3.

8¢
+ 2¢
___ ¢

4.

5¢
+ 3¢
___ ¢

5.

4¢	6¢	1¢	3¢	5¢	3¢
+ 2¢	+ 3¢	+ 7¢	+ 4¢	+ 4¢	+ 3¢
___ ¢	___ ¢	___ ¢	___ ¢	___ ¢	___ ¢

6.

1¢	1¢	4¢	3¢	6¢	1¢
+ 5¢	+ 6¢	+ 4¢	+ 7¢	+ 4¢	+ 8¢
___ ¢	___ ¢	___ ¢	___ ¢	___ ¢	___ ¢

7.

2¢	3¢	5¢	7¢	3¢	7¢
+ 2¢	+ 6¢	+ 5¢	+ 1¢	+ 2¢	+ 1¢
___ ¢	___ ¢	___ ¢	___ ¢	___ ¢	___ ¢

NUMBERS TO 20

Show the number with .
Draw and write how many.

1.

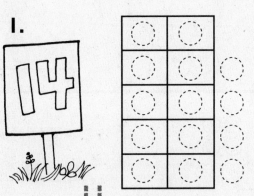

10 and __4__ more

2.

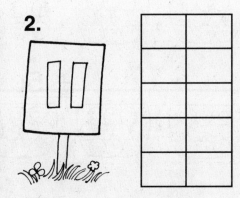

10 and _____ more

3.

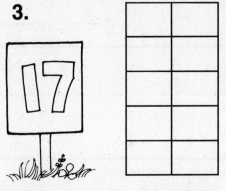

10 and _____ more

4.

10 and _____ more

5.

10 and _____ more

6.

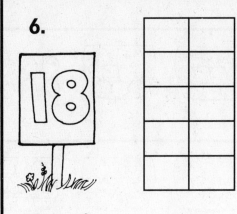

10 and _____ more

COUNT TO 50

Count. Write the number.

1.

26

_____

2.

_____

3.

_____

4.

_____

5.

_____

6.

_____

7.

_____

NUMBERS TO 50

Count tens and ones.
Write the number.

1.
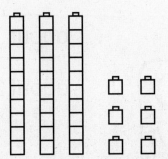

__3__ tens __6__ ones __36__

2.
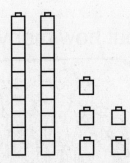

_____ tens _____ ones _____

3.
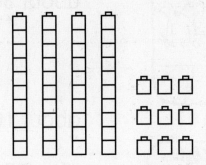

_____ tens _____ ones _____

4.
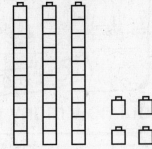

_____ tens _____ ones _____

5.
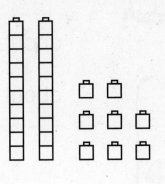

_____ tens _____ ones _____

6.
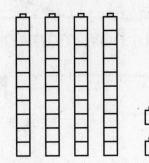

_____ tens _____ ones _____

PROBLEM-SOLVING
STRATEGY: USE ESTIMATION

✔	Read
✔	Plan
✔	Solve
✔	Look Back

Estimate to solve.

1. About how many people?

~~about 10~~

about 20

2. About how many children?

about 20

about 30

3. About how many people?

about 10

about 30

4. About how many children?

about 20

about 40

COUNT TO 100

Count. Write the number.

1. 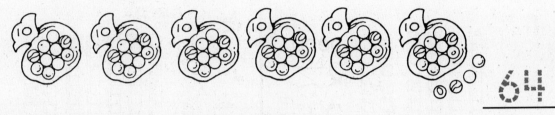 64

2. 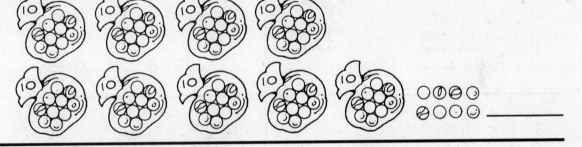 _____

3. 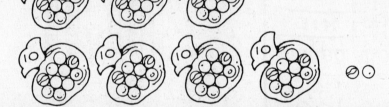 _____

4.  _____

5. 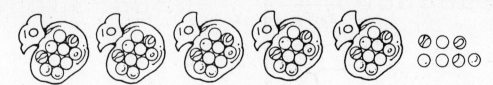 _____

NUMBERS TO 100

Count tens and ones.
Write the number.

1.

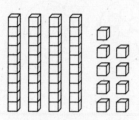

__4__ tens __9__ ones __49__

2.

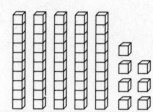

_____ tens _____ ones _____

3.

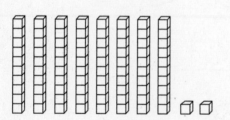

_____ tens _____ ones _____

4.

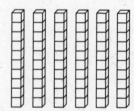

_____ tens _____ ones _____

5.

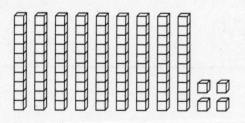

_____ tens _____ ones _____

6.

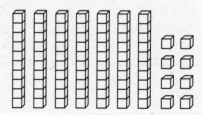

_____ tens _____ ones _____

ORDER TO 100

Write the numbers in order.

1. __9__ , __10__ , _____ , _____ , __13__ , _____ , _____ , _____

2. __21__ , __22__ , _____ , _____ , _____ , _____ , _____ , __28__

3. __39__ , _____ , __41__ , _____ , _____ , __44__ , _____ , _____

4. __57__ , _____ , _____ , _____ , __61__ , _____ , __63__ , _____

5. __70__ , __71__ , _____ , _____ , _____ , __75__ , _____ , _____

6. __83__ , _____ , _____ , __86__ , _____ , _____ , _____ , __90__

7. __92__ , _____ , __94__ , _____ , _____ , __97__ , _____ , _____

Name: _____

BEFORE, AFTER, BETWEEN

Count by ones.
Connect the dots.

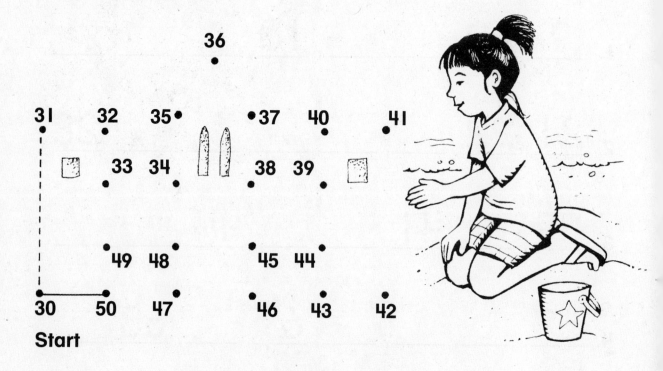

36

31   32   35   •37   40   41

33   34   38   39

49   48   45   44

30   50   47   46   43   42

Start

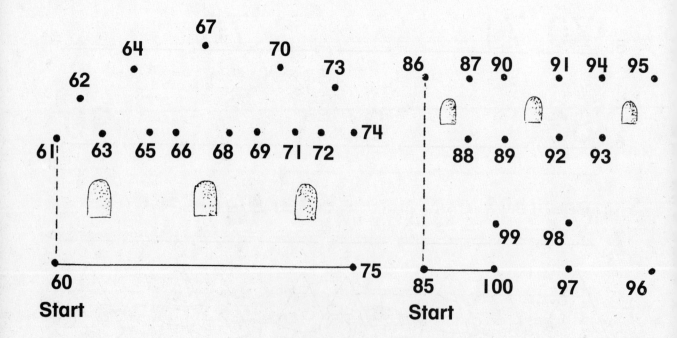

67

64   70

62   73

61   63   65   66   68   69   71   72   74

86   87   90   91   94   95

88   89   92   93

99   98

60   75   85   100   97   96

Start   **Start**

Grade 1, Chapter 6, Lesson 5, Day 2, pages 205–206

Name: _____

SKIP-COUNT

How much money? Skip-count by tens.

1.

10 , _____ , _____ , _____ , _____ _____¢

60 , _____ , _____ , _____ , _____ _____¢

How much money? Skip-count by fives.

2.

5 , _____ , _____ , _____ , _____ _____¢

30 , _____ , _____ , _____ , _____ _____¢

Skip-count by fives. Color the boxes ⟩⟩⟩ red ⟩⟩⟩ .

3.

1	2	3	4	5	6	7	8	9	10
11	12	13	14	15	16	17	18	19	20

MORE SKIP-COUNTING

Skip-count by twos.
How much money?

1.

2 , _____ , _____ , _____ , _____   _____ ¢

12 , _____ , _____ , _____ , _____   _____ ¢

Skip-count by twos. Color the boxes red.

2.

1	2	3	4	5	6	7	8	9	10
11	12	13	14	15	16	17	18	19	20
21	22	23	24	25	26	27	28	29	30
31	32	33	34	35	36	37	38	39	40
41	42	43	44	45	46	47	48	49	50

GREATER AND LESS

Ring the number that is less.

1. 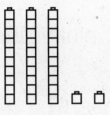   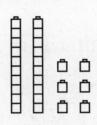

26 is **less than** 32.

    32   (26)

2. 13 11	18 21	21 12
3. 36 32	27 29	39 46

Ring the number that is greater.

4.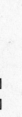

47 is **greater than** 42.

   (47)   42

5. 27 32	45 37	21 18
6. 39 41	29 26	34 43

ORDINAL NUMBERS

Start at the left. Color.

1. third [yellow]   seventh [red]   ninth [green]

2. first [green]   fourth [yellow]   eighth [red]

3. second [red]   fifth [green]   tenth [yellow]

4. fourth [green]   sixth [red]   ninth [yellow]

MIXED REVIEW

Subtract.

1.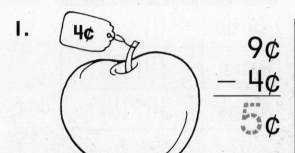

$$
\begin{array}{r}
9¢ \\
-\ 4¢ \\
\hline
5\,¢
\end{array}
$$

2.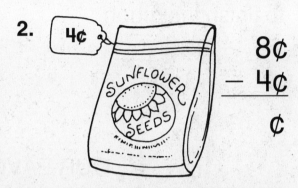

$$
\begin{array}{r}
8¢ \\
-\ 4¢ \\
\hline
¢
\end{array}
$$

3.

$$
\begin{array}{r}
10¢ \\
-\ 3¢ \\
\hline
¢
\end{array}
$$

4.

$$
\begin{array}{r}
6¢ \\
-\ 2¢ \\
\hline
¢
\end{array}
$$

5.
$$
\begin{array}{r} 9¢ \\ -\ 7¢ \\ \hline ¢ \end{array}
\qquad
\begin{array}{r} 10¢ \\ -\ 6¢ \\ \hline ¢ \end{array}
\qquad
\begin{array}{r} 3¢ \\ -\ 3¢ \\ \hline ¢ \end{array}
\qquad
\begin{array}{r} 5¢ \\ -\ 3¢ \\ \hline ¢ \end{array}
\qquad
\begin{array}{r} 8¢ \\ -\ 7¢ \\ \hline ¢ \end{array}
$$

6.
$$
\begin{array}{r} 5¢ \\ -\ 4¢ \\ \hline ¢ \end{array}
\qquad
\begin{array}{r} 7¢ \\ -\ 4¢ \\ \hline ¢ \end{array}
\qquad
\begin{array}{r} 4¢ \\ -\ 3¢ \\ \hline ¢ \end{array}
\qquad
\begin{array}{r} 6¢ \\ -\ 4¢ \\ \hline ¢ \end{array}
\qquad
\begin{array}{r} 10¢ \\ -\ 9¢ \\ \hline ¢ \end{array}
$$

7.
$$
\begin{array}{r} 8¢ \\ -\ 0¢ \\ \hline ¢ \end{array}
\qquad
\begin{array}{r} 9¢ \\ -\ 9¢ \\ \hline ¢ \end{array}
\qquad
\begin{array}{r} 7¢ \\ -\ 5¢ \\ \hline ¢ \end{array}
\qquad
\begin{array}{r} 4¢ \\ -\ 2¢ \\ \hline ¢ \end{array}
\qquad
\begin{array}{r} 6¢ \\ -\ 6¢ \\ \hline ¢ \end{array}
$$

BAR GRAPHS

Use the tally marks
to finish the graph.

OUR FAVORITE PETS	
birds	|||
cats	ℍℍℓ l
dogs	ℍℍℓ ||||

OUR FAVORITE PETS

Birds											
Cats											
Dogs											

0   1   2   3   4   5   6   7   8   9   10

1. How many votes for cats? ____6____

2. Are there more votes for birds or cats? _____

   How many more? _____

3. How many votes for dogs? _____

4. Which pet got the most votes? _____

   How do you know? _____

5. Which pet would you vote for? _____
   Add your vote to the graph.

PROBLEM SOLVING: USE A GRAPH

✔ Read
✔ Plan
✔ Solve
✔ Look Back

People Who Live in the Building

First Floor	☺ ☺ ☺ ☺ ☺ ☺
Second Floor	☺ ☺ ☺ ☺
Third Floor	☺ ☺ ☺ ☺ ☺ ☺ ☺ ☺ ☺

Each ☺ stands for 1 person.

1. Do more people live on the
   second floor or third floor?   _third_____

   How many more?   _____

2. How many people live on the
   first and second floors?   _____

3. Where do the fewest people live? _____

4. How many people live on this floor? _____

5. ✎ Write a question about the graph.

   _____

   _____

Mixed Review

Count tens and ones.
Write the number.

1.
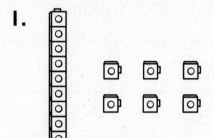

_1_ tens _6_ ones _16_

2.
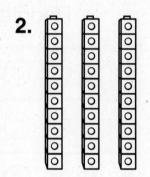
____ tens ____ ones ____

3.
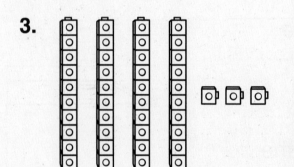
____ tens ____ ones ____

4.
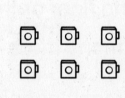
____ tens ____ ones ____

5.
____ tens ____ ones ____

6.
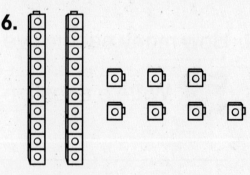
____ tens ____ ones ____

2- AND 3-DIMENSIONAL SHAPES

Color objects that make each shape.

○))) yellow)))   ▭))) purple)))   △))) red)))   ☐))) blue)))

2-DIMENSIONAL SHAPES

Count sides.
Count corners.

1.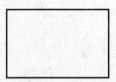

___4___ sides

___4___ corners

2.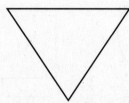

_____ sides

_____ corners

3.

_____ sides

_____ corners

4.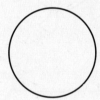

_____ sides

_____ corners

5.

_____ sides

_____ corners

6.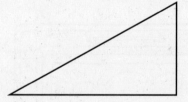

_____ sides

_____ corners

PROBLEM-SOLVING STRATEGY: USE A PHYSICAL MODEL

✔ Read
✔ Plan
✔ Solve
✔ Look Back

Use ⊠ to solve.

Draw lines to show your answer.

1. Ben made this kite.
Show how he did it.

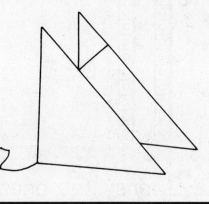

2. Kimi made this kite.
Show how she did it.

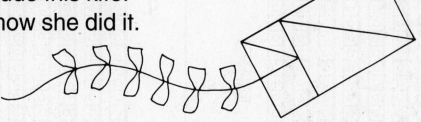

3. Grace made this kite.
Show how she did it.

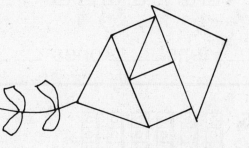

4. William made this flower kite.
Show how he did it.

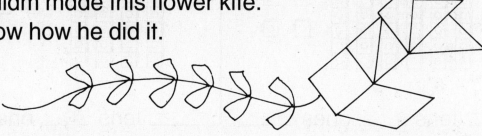

MIXED REVIEW

Count tens and ones.
Write the number.

1.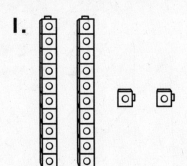

_2_ tens _2_ ones _22_

2.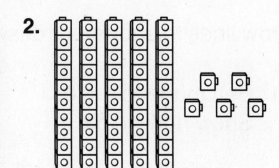

___ tens ___ ones ___

3.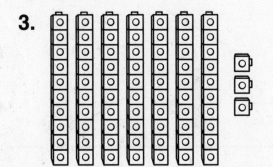

___ tens ___ ones ___

4.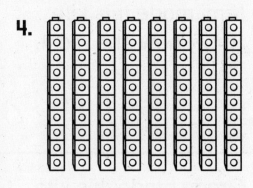

___ tens ___ ones ___

5.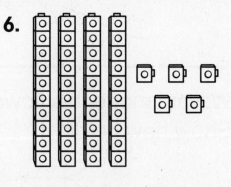

___ tens ___ ones ___

6.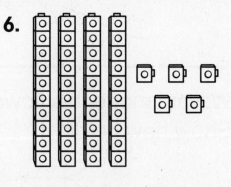

___ tens ___ ones ___

Grade 1, Chapter 7, Lesson 4, Day 1, pages 245–246

Name: _____

HALVES

Color $\frac{1}{2}$.

Only color the kites that show halves.

1.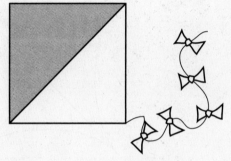

2.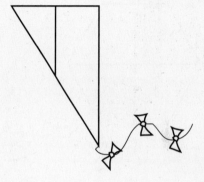

3.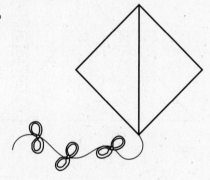

4.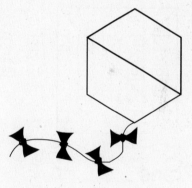

5.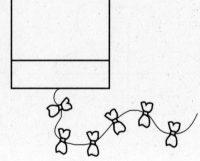

6.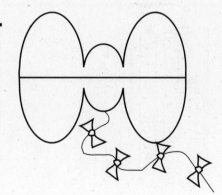

FOURTHS

Color $\frac{1}{4}$.

Only color the kites that show fourths.

1.

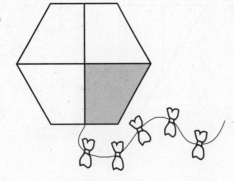

2.

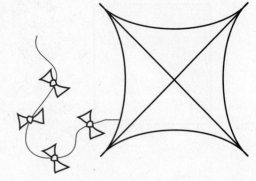

3.

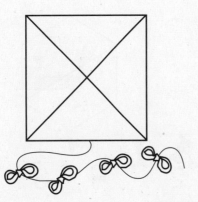

4.

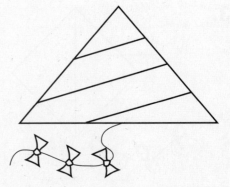

5.

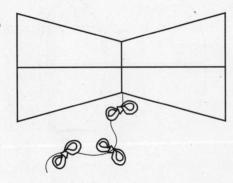

6.

THIRDS

Ring the fraction.

1.

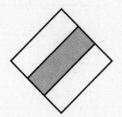 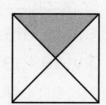 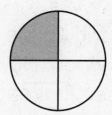

$\frac{1}{4}$ $\left(\frac{1}{3}\right)$ $\frac{1}{2}$ $\qquad$ $\frac{1}{4}$ $\frac{1}{3}$ $\frac{1}{2}$ $\qquad$ $\frac{1}{4}$ $\frac{1}{3}$ $\frac{1}{2}$

2.

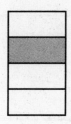  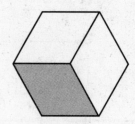

$\frac{1}{4}$ $\frac{1}{3}$ $\frac{1}{2}$ $\qquad$ $\frac{1}{4}$ $\frac{1}{3}$ $\frac{1}{2}$ $\qquad$ $\frac{1}{4}$ $\frac{1}{3}$ $\frac{1}{2}$

3.

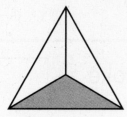 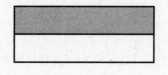 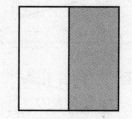

$\frac{1}{4}$ $\frac{1}{3}$ $\frac{1}{2}$ $\qquad$ $\frac{1}{4}$ $\frac{1}{3}$ $\frac{1}{2}$ $\qquad$ $\frac{1}{4}$ $\frac{1}{3}$ $\frac{1}{2}$

PROBLEM SOLVING: DRAW A PICTURE

✔	Read
✔	Plan
✔	Solve
✔	Look Back

Draw a picture to solve.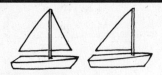

1. Mr. Jones makes 2 sailboats from wood. How can he divide the wood so that each boat gets an equal part?

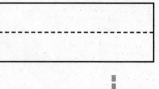

How much wood does each boat get? _____

2. How can this piece of wood be divided to make 3 sailboats?

How much wood does each boat get? _____

3. Mr. Jones cuts a circle to make 4 sails. Show how he can divide the wood so that each sail gets an equal part.

How much wood does each sail get? _____

4. What if Mr. Jones cuts a square to make 2 sails? Show how he can divide the wood so that each sail gets an equal part.

How much wood does each sail get? _____

PENNIES AND NICKELS

Count. Write how much money.

1. 1¢   2¢   3¢   4¢   5¢

2.   _____

3.   _____

4.   _____

5.   _____

6.   _____

PENNIES AND DIMES

Count. Write how much money.

1.  10¢ 11¢ 12¢ 13¢   13¢
_____

2.

_____

3.

_____

4.

_____

5.

_____

6.

_____

MIXED REVIEW

Color objects that make each shape.

MORE COUNTING MONEY

Mark the coins that show the price.

1.
22¢

2.
36¢

3.
40¢

4.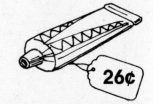
26¢

5.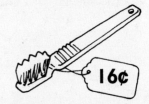
16¢

6.
35¢

PROBLEM-SOLVING STRATEGY: GUESS AND TEST

Guess and test to solve.
Which 2 items does each child buy?

I. Lin spends 6¢.

2. José spends 5¢.

3. Max spends 9¢.

4. Sue spends 7¢.

5. Jan spends 4¢.

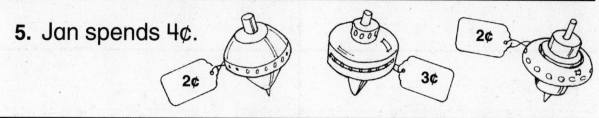

6. Bo spends 10¢.

QUARTERS

Count. Write how much money.

1.

2.

_____

3.

_____

4.

_____

5.

_____

6.

_____

7.

_____

8.

_____

MIXED REVIEW

Ring the fraction.

1.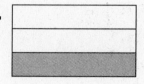

$\dfrac{1}{4}$ ⦅$\dfrac{1}{3}$⦆ $\dfrac{1}{2}$

2.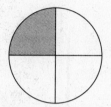

$\dfrac{1}{4}$ $\dfrac{1}{3}$ $\dfrac{1}{2}$

3.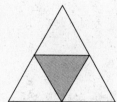

$\dfrac{1}{4}$ $\dfrac{1}{3}$ $\dfrac{1}{2}$

4.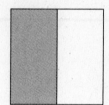

$\dfrac{1}{4}$ $\dfrac{1}{3}$ $\dfrac{1}{2}$

5.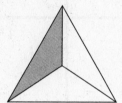

$\dfrac{1}{4}$ $\dfrac{1}{3}$ $\dfrac{1}{2}$

6.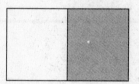

$\dfrac{1}{4}$ $\dfrac{1}{3}$ $\dfrac{1}{2}$

7.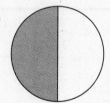

$\dfrac{1}{4}$ $\dfrac{1}{3}$ $\dfrac{1}{2}$

8.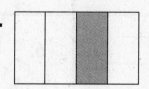

$\dfrac{1}{4}$ $\dfrac{1}{3}$ $\dfrac{1}{2}$

9.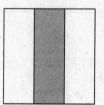

$\dfrac{1}{4}$ $\dfrac{1}{3}$ $\dfrac{1}{2}$

MORE COMPARING MONEY

Write how much. Compare.
Which is **less** money?

1.

 15¢

20¢

2.

 _____

_____

3.

 _____

 _____

4.

 _____

_____

5.

_____

_____

6.

_____

 _____

PROBLEM SOLVING: USE DATA FROM A TABLE

✔ Read
✔ Plan
✔ Solve
✔ Look Back

Use the table to solve.
Write **yes** or **no**.

SCHOOL STORE	
Item	**Price**
eraser	28¢
ruler	47¢
marker	16¢
pencil	12¢
tape	30¢

1. You have .

   Do you have enough
   money to buy an eraser?

   No

2. You have .

   Do you have enough
   money to buy a pencil?

   _____

3. You have .

   Do you have enough
   money to buy a
   marker?

   _____

4. You have 27¢.

   Can you buy tape?

   _____

5. You have 35¢.

   Can you buy a ruler?

   _____

Name:

MIXED REVIEW

Count the coins.
Match to a price.

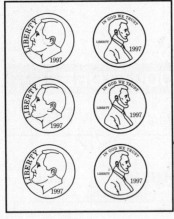

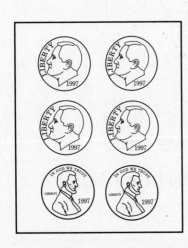

Fruit Prices	
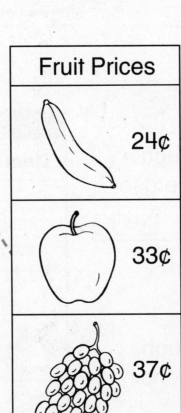	24¢
	33¢
	37¢
	16¢
	21¢
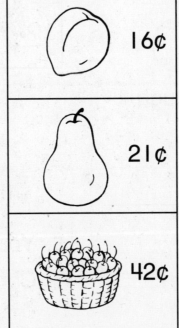	42¢

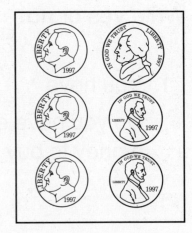

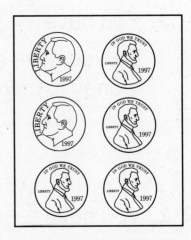

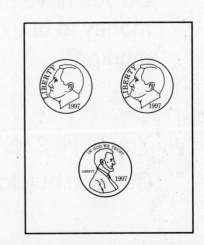

Grade 1, Chapter 9, Lesson 1, Day 1, pages 299–300

HOUR

Show the time on a 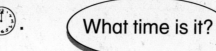.
Then write the time.

What time is it?

1.

_____ o'clock

2.

_____ o'clock

3.

_____ o'clock

4.

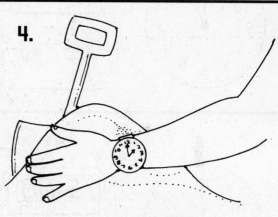

_____ o'clock

5.

_____ o'clock

6.

_____ o'clock

Name: _____

TIME TO THE HOUR

Write the time.

1.

8:00

2.

___:___

3.

___:___

4.

___:___

5.

___:___

6.

___:___

7.
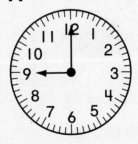

___:___

8.

___:___

Name: _____

HALF HOUR

Show the time on a 🕐.
Then write the time.

1.

6:30
___

2.

:
___

3.

:
___

4.

:
___

5.

:
___

6.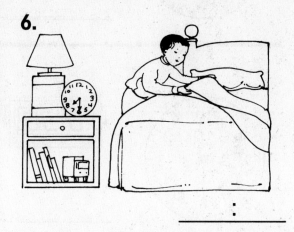

:
___

TIME TO THE HALF HOUR

Write the time.

1.

2.

`4:30`

___ : ___

3.

`7:30`

___ : ___

4.

`10:30`

___ : ___

5.

`3:30`

___ : ___

6.

`1:30`

___ : ___

7.

`8:30`

___ : ___

8.
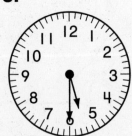

`5:30`

___ : ___

PROBLEM-SOLVING STRATEGY: MAKE A LIST

✔ Read
✔ Plan
✔ Solve
✔ Look Back

Color to make a list.

1. Kerri has these flowers and pots. Show the different ways she can put the flowers in the pots.

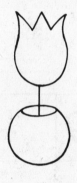   

2. Sam wants to make a peanut-butter-and-jelly sandwich. Show the different sandwiches he can make.

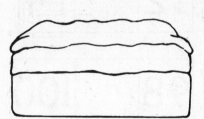 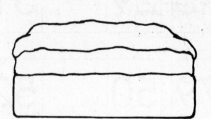 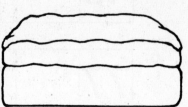

MIXED REVIEW

Write the number that comes just before.

1.  | 53 | 31 | 86

2. | 14 | 99 | 20

Write the number that comes just after.

3. 27 | 10 | 49 |

4. 33 | 60 | 82 |

Write the number that comes between.

5. 43 | | 45   29 | | 31   12 | | 14

6. 77 | | 79   50 | | 52   98 | | 100

Practice (89)

MORE ABOUT CALENDARS

SEPTEMBER						
Sunday	Monday	Tuesday	Wednesday	Thursday	Friday	Saturday
		1	2	3	4	5
6	7 Labor Day	8	9 First day of school	10	11	12
13 Grandparent's Day	14	15	16	17	18	19
20	21	22 First day of fall	23	24	25 Library	26
27	28	29	30			

Use the calendar to solve.

1. What is the date of Labor Day?

   September 7

2. What date is the first day of fall?

   _____

3. What day of the week is Grandparent's Day?

   _____

4. What day of the week is the first day of school?

   _____

PROBLEM SOLVING: USE ESTIMATION

Solve.

1. About how long can she stand on her head?

(I minute)   I hour

2. About how long for a birthday party?

2 minutes   2 hours

3. About how long to wait for a stoplight?

2 minutes   2 hours

4. About how long to blow up a balloon?

I minute   I hour

5. About how long to make a bed?

3 minutes   3 hours

6. About how long to walk to school?

4 minutes   4 hours

Name: _____

DOUBLES

Add or subtract.

1.

$$8 + 8 = 16$$

$$16 - 8 = 8$$

2.

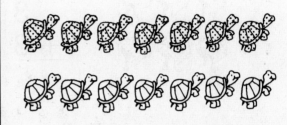

$$7 + 7 = $$

$$14 - 7 = $$

Color double addition facts red .
Color double subtraction facts blue .

3.

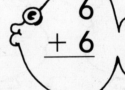 $$5 + 5$$ $$8 - 4$$ $$6 + 6$$ $$10 - 5$$

$$16 - 8$$ $$2 + 2$$ $$14 - 7$$ $$7 + 7$$

 $$4 + 4$$ $$8 + 8$$ $$6 - 3$$ $$18 - 9$$

Name: _____

DOUBLES PLUS 1

Add.

1.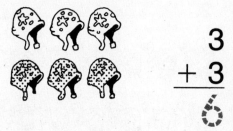

$$\begin{array}{r} 3 \\ + 3 \\ \hline 6 \end{array}$$

$$\begin{array}{r} 3 \\ + 4 \\ \hline 7 \end{array}$$

2.

$$\begin{array}{r} 5 \\ + 5 \\ \hline \end{array}$$

$$\begin{array}{r} 5 \\ + 6 \\ \hline \end{array}$$

Color double facts (green).
Color double plus one facts (yellow).

3.
$$\begin{array}{r} 3 \\ + 2 \\ \hline \end{array}$$
$$\begin{array}{r} 7 \\ + 7 \\ \hline \end{array}$$
$$\begin{array}{r} 6 \\ + 7 \\ \hline \end{array}$$
$$\begin{array}{r} 3 \\ + 3 \\ \hline \end{array}$$

$$\begin{array}{r} 9 \\ + 8 \\ \hline \end{array}$$
$$\begin{array}{r} 2 \\ + 2 \\ \hline \end{array}$$
$$\begin{array}{r} 8 \\ + 7 \\ \hline \end{array}$$
$$\begin{array}{r} 4 \\ + 4 \\ \hline \end{array}$$

$$\begin{array}{r} 5 \\ + 4 \\ \hline \end{array}$$
$$\begin{array}{r} 9 \\ + 9 \\ \hline \end{array}$$
$$\begin{array}{r} 4 \\ + 3 \\ \hline \end{array}$$
$$\begin{array}{r} 8 \\ + 9 \\ \hline \end{array}$$

Grade 1, Chapter 10, Lesson 1, Day 2, pages 337–338

MIXED REVIEW

Count tens and ones.
Write the number.

1.

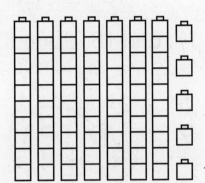

_7_ tens _5_ ones _75_

2.

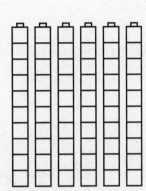

___ tens ___ ones ___

3.

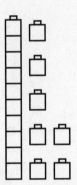

___ tens ___ ones ___

4.

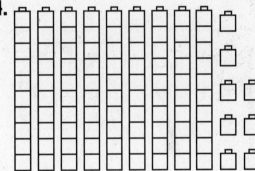

___ tens ___ ones ___

5.

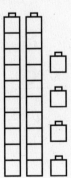

___ tens ___ ones ___

6.

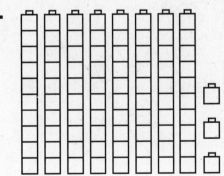

___ tens ___ ones ___

Name: _____

ADD

Add. Color the area.

11 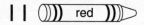 red   12))) yellow   13))) orange

14 and 15))) blue   16, 17, and 18))) green

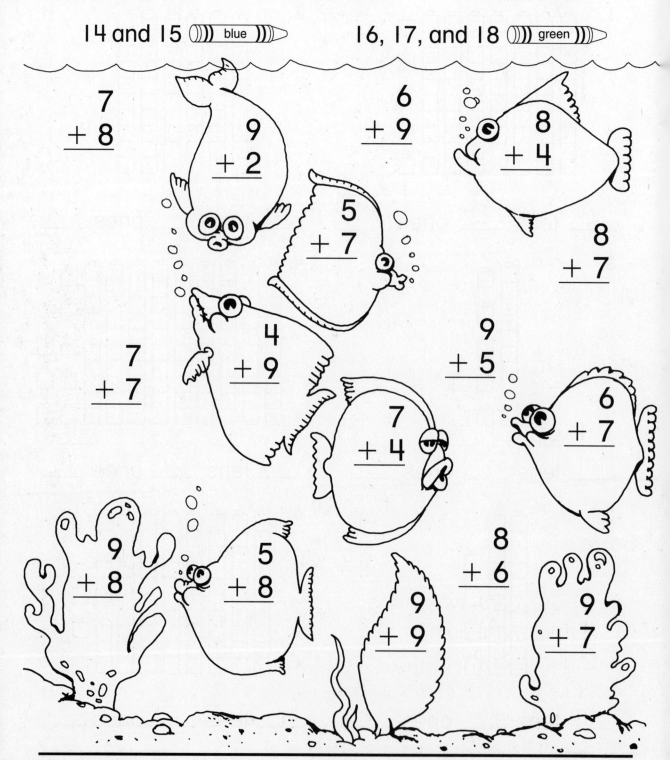

7
+ 8

9
+ 2

6
+ 9

8
+ 4

5
+ 7

8
+ 7

7
+ 7

4
+ 9

9
+ 5

7
+ 4

6
+ 7

9
+ 8

5
+ 8

8
+ 6

9
+ 9

9
+ 7

ADD THREE NUMBERS

Find the sum.

1.
$$
\begin{array}{r} 3 \\ 6 \\ +\ 4 \\ \hline 13 \end{array}
\qquad
\begin{array}{r} 4 \\ 8 \\ +\ 4 \\ \hline \end{array}
\qquad
\begin{array}{r} 2 \\ 7 \\ +\ 7 \\ \hline \end{array}
\qquad
\begin{array}{r} 3¢ \\ 6¢ \\ +\ 4¢ \\ \hline \end{array}
\qquad
\begin{array}{r} 5 \\ 5 \\ +\ 5 \\ \hline \end{array}
\qquad
\begin{array}{r} 7 \\ 1 \\ +\ 6 \\ \hline \end{array}
$$

2.
$$
\begin{array}{r} 2 \\ 3 \\ +\ 8 \\ \hline \end{array}
\qquad
\begin{array}{r} 3 \\ 3 \\ +\ 7 \\ \hline \end{array}
\qquad
\begin{array}{r} 6¢ \\ 3¢ \\ +\ 1¢ \\ \hline \end{array}
\qquad
\begin{array}{r} 4 \\ 5 \\ +\ 9 \\ \hline \end{array}
\qquad
\begin{array}{r} 6 \\ 0 \\ +\ 6 \\ \hline \end{array}
\qquad
\begin{array}{r} 7 \\ 1 \\ +\ 5 \\ \hline \end{array}
$$

3.
$$
\begin{array}{r} 4¢ \\ 3¢ \\ +\ 6¢ \\ \hline \end{array}
\qquad
\begin{array}{r} 2 \\ 7 \\ +\ 5 \\ \hline \end{array}
\qquad
\begin{array}{r} 3 \\ 3 \\ +\ 4 \\ \hline \end{array}
\qquad
\begin{array}{r} 7 \\ 2 \\ +\ 6 \\ \hline \end{array}
\qquad
\begin{array}{r} 8 \\ 2 \\ +\ 6 \\ \hline \end{array}
\qquad
\begin{array}{r} 5 \\ 0 \\ +\ 7 \\ \hline \end{array}
$$

Solve.

4. 6 ducks are swimming.
4 ducks are flying.
2 ducks are walking.
How many ducks are
there in all?   _____ ducks

Workspace

Name: _____

MIXED REVIEW

Write the time.

1.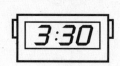

 _____ : _____

2.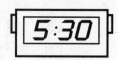

_____ : _____

3.

_____ : _____

4.

_____ : _____

5. 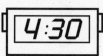

_____ : _____

6.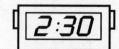

_____ : _____

7. 

_____ : _____

8. 

_____ : _____

SUBTRACT

Subtract.

1. $\begin{array}{r} 11 \\ -\ 3 \\ \hline 8 \end{array}$ $\quad$ $\begin{array}{r} 11 \\ -\ 8 \\ \hline 3 \end{array}$ ○○○ ○○○ ○○ $\qquad$ 2. $\begin{array}{r} 13 \\ -\ 4 \\ \hline \end{array}$ $\quad$ $\begin{array}{r} 13 \\ -\ 9 \\ \hline \end{array}$ ○○○○ ○○○ ○○○

3. $\begin{array}{r} 11 \\ -\ 5 \\ \hline \end{array}$ $\begin{array}{r} 13¢ \\ -\ 6¢ \\ \hline \end{array}$ $\begin{array}{r} 12 \\ -\ 9 \\ \hline \end{array}$ $\begin{array}{r} 13¢ \\ -\ 7¢ \\ \hline \end{array}$ $\begin{array}{r} 11 \\ -\ 6 \\ \hline \end{array}$ $\begin{array}{r} 13¢ \\ -\ 5¢ \\ \hline \end{array}$

4. $\begin{array}{r} 12 \\ -\ 3 \\ \hline \end{array}$ $\begin{array}{r} 11¢ \\ -\ 4¢ \\ \hline \end{array}$ $\begin{array}{r} 13¢ \\ -\ 8¢ \\ \hline \end{array}$ $\begin{array}{r} 12 \\ -\ 8 \\ \hline \end{array}$ $\begin{array}{r} 11¢ \\ -\ 2¢ \\ \hline \end{array}$ $\begin{array}{r} 12 \\ -\ 4 \\ \hline \end{array}$

Solve.

Workspace

5. 13 ducks are floating on the water. 6 ducks fly away. How many ducks are left on the water?

_____ ducks

6. 11 gulls are sitting on the dock. 7 gulls fly away. How many gulls are left on the dock?

_____ gulls

MORE SUBTRACTING

Subtract.

1.

$$15 - 8 = 7$$

$$15 - 7 = 8$$

2.

$$14 - 5$$ $$17 - 8$$ $$14 - 7$$ $$16¢ - 9¢$$ $$12 - 6$$ $$14 - 8$$

3.

$$15 - 6$$ $$14 - 9$$ $$16¢ - 7¢$$ $$15 - 9$$ $$17 - 9$$ $$15 - 7$$

Solve.

Workspace

4. Ben found 15 shells.
He gave 6 of the shells away.
How many shells does Ben have left?

_____ shells

5. Write a subtraction word problem.
Have a partner solve it.
Use your own paper.

PROBLEM-SOLVING STRATEGY:
CHOOSE THE OPERATION

Choose **add** or **subtract.** Solve.

Workspace

1. Rosa buys a fish for 9¢. Then she buys a snail for 8¢. How much money does Rosa spend?

   add   subtract   _____¢

2. There are 15 fish in a tank. 8 are guppies and the rest are goldfish. How many goldfish are in the tank?

   add   subtract   _____ goldfish

3. The store has 9 big fish tanks and 5 small fish tanks. How many fish tanks are in the store?

   add   subtract   _____ fish tanks

4. Chris buys 15 fish. Paul buys 7 fish. How many more fish does Chris buy than Paul?

   add   subtract   _____ fish

ADD AND SUBTRACT

Add or subtract. Use ⬤◯ if you want to.

1.

$$\begin{array}{r} 5 \\ + 6 \\ \hline 11 \end{array} \qquad \begin{array}{r} 11 \\ - 6 \\ \hline 5 \end{array}$$

2.

$$\begin{array}{r} 8 \\ + 5 \\ \hline \end{array} \qquad \begin{array}{r} 13 \\ - 5 \\ \hline \end{array}$$

3.

$$\begin{array}{r} 4 \\ + 7 \\ \hline \end{array} \qquad \begin{array}{r} 11 \\ - 7 \\ \hline \end{array} \qquad \begin{array}{r} 6 \\ + 7 \\ \hline \end{array} \qquad \begin{array}{r} 13 \\ - 7 \\ \hline \end{array} \qquad \begin{array}{r} 9¢ \\ + 3¢ \\ \hline \end{array} \qquad \begin{array}{r} 12¢ \\ - 3¢ \\ \hline \end{array}$$

4.

$$\begin{array}{r} 7 \\ + 8 \\ \hline \end{array} \qquad \begin{array}{r} 15 \\ - 8 \\ \hline \end{array} \qquad \begin{array}{r} 6¢ \\ + 8¢ \\ \hline \end{array} \qquad \begin{array}{r} 14¢ \\ - 8¢ \\ \hline \end{array} \qquad \begin{array}{r} 2 \\ + 9 \\ \hline \end{array} \qquad \begin{array}{r} 11 \\ - 9 \\ \hline \end{array}$$

5.

$$\begin{array}{r} 8 \\ + 8 \\ \hline \end{array} \qquad \begin{array}{r} 16 \\ - 8 \\ \hline \end{array} \qquad \begin{array}{r} 9 \\ + 8 \\ \hline \end{array} \qquad \begin{array}{r} 17 \\ - 8 \\ \hline \end{array} \qquad \begin{array}{r} 7¢ \\ + 5¢ \\ \hline \end{array} \qquad \begin{array}{r} 12¢ \\ - 5¢ \\ \hline \end{array}$$

FACT FAMILIES

Complete the fact family.

1.

$5 + 7 = \underline{12}$

$7 + 5 = \underline{12}$

$12 - 7 = \underline{5}$

$12 - 5 = \underline{7}$

2.

$7 + 6 = \underline{\quad}$

$6 + 7 = \underline{\quad}$

$13 - 6 = \underline{\quad}$

$13 - 7 = \underline{\quad}$

3.

$9 + 7 = \underline{\quad}$

$7 + 9 = \underline{\quad}$

$16 - 7 = \underline{\quad}$

$16 - 9 = \underline{\quad}$

4.

$5 + 6 = \underline{\quad}$

$6 + 5 = \underline{\quad}$

$11 - 6 = \underline{\quad}$

$11 - 5 = \underline{\quad}$

5.

$8 + 7 = \underline{\quad}$

$7 + 8 = \underline{\quad}$

$15 - 7 = \underline{\quad}$

$15 - 8 = \underline{\quad}$

6.

$4 + 9 = \underline{\quad}$

$9 + 4 = \underline{\quad}$

$13 - 9 = \underline{\quad}$

$13 - 4 = \underline{\quad}$

PROBLEM SOLVING: CHOOSE A STRATEGY

Show how you solve these problems.

Workspace

1. Bria found 9 shells.
   Cody found 6 shells.
   How many shells did Bria
   and Cody find in all? _____ shells

2. Dan saw 12 gulls.
   Jen saw 8 gulls.
   How many more gulls
   did Dan see than Jen? _____ gulls

3. 8¢   7¢   5¢

   Anita buys a fish and a shell.
   How much money does
   she spend? _____ ¢

4. 🐚   🫘   🐚

   Paul has these shells.
   He wants to give 2 away.
   How many ways can he
   match them? _____ ways

MIXED REVIEW

Add or subtract.

1.

$$\begin{array}{r} 7 \\ +\ 6 \\ \hline 13 \end{array} \qquad \begin{array}{r} 13 \\ -\ 6 \\ \hline 7 \end{array}$$

2.

$$\begin{array}{r} 3 \\ +\ 8 \\ \hline \end{array} \qquad \begin{array}{r} 11 \\ -\ 8 \\ \hline \end{array}$$

Add or subtract. Use ☐ if you want to.

3.
$$\begin{array}{r} 7 \\ +\ 5 \\ \hline \end{array} \quad \begin{array}{r} 12 \\ -\ 5 \\ \hline \end{array} \quad \begin{array}{r} 9 \\ +\ 8 \\ \hline \end{array} \quad \begin{array}{r} 17 \\ -\ 8 \\ \hline \end{array} \quad \begin{array}{r} 6 \\ +\ 6 \\ \hline \end{array} \quad \begin{array}{r} 12 \\ -\ 6 \\ \hline \end{array}$$

4.
$$\begin{array}{r} 4 \\ +\ 9 \\ \hline \end{array} \quad \begin{array}{r} 13 \\ -\ 9 \\ \hline \end{array} \quad \begin{array}{r} 7 \\ +\ 7 \\ \hline \end{array} \quad \begin{array}{r} 14 \\ -\ 7 \\ \hline \end{array} \quad \begin{array}{r} 2 \\ +\ 9 \\ \hline \end{array} \quad \begin{array}{r} 11 \\ -\ 9 \\ \hline \end{array}$$

5.
$$\begin{array}{r} 8 \\ +\ 8 \\ \hline \end{array} \quad \begin{array}{r} 16 \\ -\ 8 \\ \hline \end{array} \quad \begin{array}{r} 6 \\ +\ 5 \\ \hline \end{array} \quad \begin{array}{r} 11 \\ -\ 5 \\ \hline \end{array} \quad \begin{array}{r} 7 \\ +\ 4 \\ \hline \end{array} \quad \begin{array}{r} 11 \\ -\ 4 \\ \hline \end{array}$$

Name: _____

MEASURE LENGTH

Estimate how long.
Then measure with 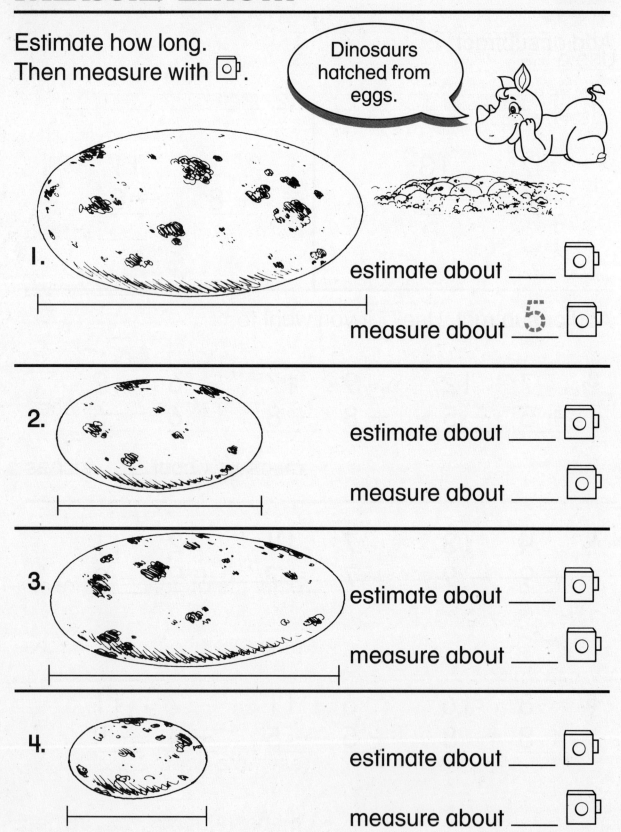.

Dinosaurs hatched from eggs.

1.

estimate about ____

measure about __5__

2.

estimate about ____

measure about ____

3.

estimate about ____

measure about ____

4.

estimate about ____

measure about ____

Name: _____

INCH

Use a 0 inches 1 2 3 4 5 6 .
Estimate how long.
Then measure.

1.

estimate about ____ inches

measure about __4.4__ inches

2.

estimate about ____ inches

measure about ____ inches

3.

estimate about ____ inches

measure about ____ inches

4.

estimate about ____ inches

measure about ____ inches

Name: _____

FOOT

Use a [ruler: 0 inches 1 2 3 4 5 6] .
Find the real object.
Estimate how long.
Then measure and choose the
best answer.

	Estimate	Measure
1.	(less than 1 foot) more than 1 foot	less than 1 foot more than 1 foot
2.	less than 1 foot more than 1 foot	less than 1 foot more than 1 foot
3.	less than 1 foot more than 1 foot	less than 1 foot more than 1 foot
4.	less than 1 foot more than 1 foot	less than 1 foot more than 1 foot

CENTIMETER

Use a ![ruler](0 1 2 3 4 5 6 7 8 9 10 11 12 13 14 15 16 centimeters).
Estimate how long.
Then measure.

1.

estimate about _____ cm   measure about ⦙⦙ cm

2.

estimate about _____ cm   measure about _____ cm

3.

estimate about _____ cm   measure about _____ cm

4.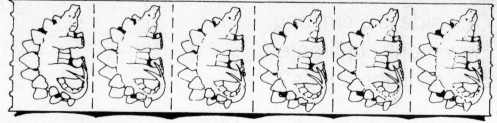

estimate about _____ cm   measure about _____ cm

PROBLEM-SOLVING STRATEGY: DRAW A PICTURE

Draw a picture to solve.

1. Sara draws a square around a picture. The square is 5 cm on one side. How many centimeters around is the square?

_5_ + ___ + ___ + ___ = ___ cm around

2. Ben draws a rectangle around a picture. One side is 4 cm. Another side is 7 cm. How many centimeters around is the rectangle?

___ + ___ + ___ + ___ = ___ cm around

3. Mika draws a rectangle. One side is 2 cm long. One side is 6 cm long. How many centimeters around is the shape?

___ + ___ + ___ + ___ = ___ cm around

POUND

Estimate.
Which things weigh less than 1 pound?

1.

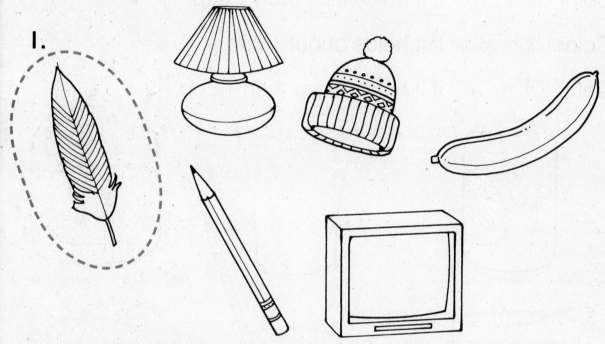

Which things weigh more than 1 pound?

2.

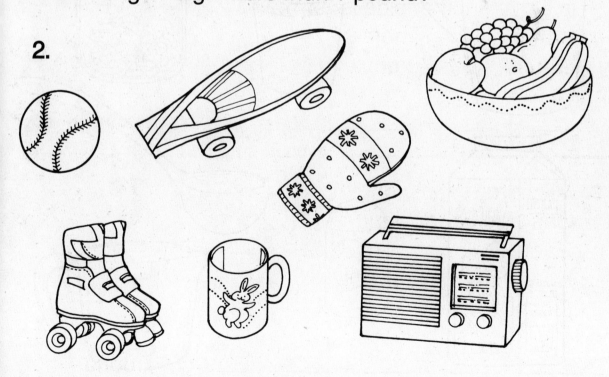

Name: _____

CUP

Estimate.

Color (green) if it holds less than 1 cup.

Color (orange) if it holds about 1 cup.

Color (blue) if it holds more than 1 cup.

MIXED REVIEW

Count. Write how much money.

1.

35¢

2.

_____

3.

_____

4.

_____

5.

_____

6.

_____

7.

_____

8.

_____

PROBLEM SOLVING: CHOOSE REASONABLE ANSWERS

✔ Read
✔ Plan
✔ Solve
✔ Look Back

Ring the answer that makes sense.

1. Emma builds a snowman.

   About what temperature is it?

   20 cups   (20°F)

2. Len weighs 60 pounds.

   About how much does Sam weigh?

   10 pounds   50 pounds

3. Dakota throws the ball.

   About how far does the ball go?

   30 feet   30 inches

MIXED REVIEW

Use a  .
Estimate how long.
Then measure.

Remember to start at 0.

1.

estimate about _____ inches

measure about __2__ inches

2.

estimate about _____ inches

measure about _____ inches

3.

estimate about _____ inches

measure about _____ inches

4.

estimate about _____ inches

measure about _____ inches

Name: _____

ADD FACTS AND TENS

Add.

Use ▢ if you want to.

1. $3 + 3 =$ __6__ $5 + 3 =$ ___

    $30 + 30 =$ __60__ $50 + 30 =$ ___

2. $2 + 7 =$ ___ $5 + 1 =$ ___

    $20 + 70 =$ ___ $50 + 10 =$ ___

3. $2 + 2 =$ ___ $3 + 4 =$ ___

    $20 + 20 =$ ___ $30 + 40 =$ ___

4. $15 + 2 =$ ___ $17 + 3 =$ ___

5. $30 + 3 =$ ___ $63 + 1 =$ ___

6. $26 + 2 =$ ___ $42 + 3 =$ ___

7. $41 + 3 =$ ___ $36 + 1 =$ ___

8. $62 + 1 =$ ___ $53 + 2 =$ ___

9. $54 + 3 =$ ___ $27 + 2 =$ ___

COUNT ON BY TENS

Count on by tens to add.

Use ☐ or ▦ if you want to.

1. $23 + 30 =$ __53__

2. $32 + 10 =$ ____

3. $52 + 20 =$ ____   4. $47 + 30 =$ ____

5. $76 + 10 =$ ____   6. $16 + 20 =$ ____

7. $44 + 30 =$ ____   8. $23 + 10 =$ ____

9. $17 + 20 =$ ____   10. $67 + 30 =$ ____

Solve.   **Workspace**

11. 23 children play flutes.
    10 children play drums.
    How many children is
    that in all?

    $23 + 10 = 33$

    _____ children

12. 34 girls sing.
    20 boys join them.
    How many boys
    and girls sing?

    _____ boys and girls

2-DIGIT ADDITION

Add.

Use ▭▭▭ or ⬜
if you want to.

1. $36 + 5 = \underline{41}$

2. $63 + 4 = \underline{}$

3. $22 + 6 = \underline{}$

4. $34 + 8 = \underline{}$

5. $61 + 8 = \underline{}$

6. $47 + 3 = \underline{}$

7. $17 + 2 = \underline{}$

8. $35 + 3 = \underline{}$

9. $48 + 6 = \underline{}$

10. $54 + 2 = \underline{}$

11. $36 + 9 = \underline{}$

12. $13 + 6 = \underline{}$

Solve.

Workspace

13. Nina needs 15 red shirts and 8 green shirts for the show. How many shirts does she need?

$$15 + 8 = 23$$

_____ shirts

14. 22 children brought costumes. 8 children made tickets. How many children is that in all?

_____ children

MORE ADDITION

Add. Use models to help.

1. $17 + 23 = $ _**40**_   2. $36 + 18 = $ _____

3. $26 + 52 = $ _____   4. $14 + 13 = $ _____

5. $47 + 18 = $ _____   6. $41 + 14 = $ _____

7. $27 + 22 = $ _____   8. $30 + 12 = $ _____

9. $43 + 25 = $ _____   10. $16 + 37 = $ _____

11. $25 + 25 = $ _____   12. $47 + 28 = $ _____

13. $12 + 18 = $ _____   14. $38 + 16 = $ _____

15. $32 + 37 = $ _____   16. $15 + 12 = $ _____

17. $57 + 19 = $ _____   18. $34 + 43 = $ _____

19. $34 + 32 = $ _____   20. $43 + 17 = $ _____

21. $55 + 27 = $ _____   22. $19 + 28 = $ _____

23. $36 + 36 = $ _____   24. $48 + 33 = $ _____

PROBLEM-SOLVING STRATEGY: USE ESTIMATION

Solve.
Use estimation.

Use the number line to find the ten.

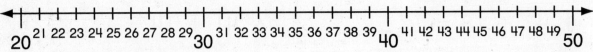

20 21 22 23 24 25 26 27 28 29 30 31 32 33 34 35 36 37 38 39 40 41 42 43 44 45 46 47 48 49 50

1. Dena buys a pencil for 23¢.
   Tim buys a ruler for 38¢.
   About how much do they spend?

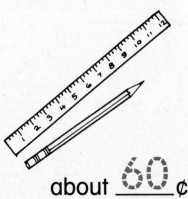

   20 + 40 = 60   about 60 ¢

2. Mark pays 28¢ for stickers.
   He pays 43¢ for a mask.
   About how much does he pay in all?

   ___ + ___ = ___   about ___ ¢

3. Rosa spends 32¢ for rubber bands.
   She spends 48¢ for a bow.
   About how much does she spend in all?

   ___ + ___ = ___   about ___ ¢

MIXED REVIEW

Subtract.

1.

$$\begin{array}{r} 12 \\ -\ 5 \\ \hline 7 \end{array}$$ $$\begin{array}{r} 12 \\ -\ 7 \\ \hline 5 \end{array}$$

2.

$$\begin{array}{r} 14 \\ -\ 6 \\ \hline \end{array}$$ $$\begin{array}{r} 14 \\ -\ 8 \\ \hline \end{array}$$

3. $$\begin{array}{r} 13 \\ -\ 7 \\ \hline \end{array}$$ $$\begin{array}{r} 15¢ \\ -\ 8¢ \\ \hline \end{array}$$ $$\begin{array}{r} 11 \\ -\ 8 \\ \hline \end{array}$$ $$\begin{array}{r} 13¢ \\ -\ 6¢ \\ \hline \end{array}$$ $$\begin{array}{r} 12 \\ -\ 6 \\ \hline \end{array}$$ $$\begin{array}{r} 16¢ \\ -\ 7¢ \\ \hline \end{array}$$

4. $$\begin{array}{r} 14 \\ -\ 9 \\ \hline \end{array}$$ $$\begin{array}{r} 11¢ \\ -\ 3¢ \\ \hline \end{array}$$ $$\begin{array}{r} 13¢ \\ -\ 7¢ \\ \hline \end{array}$$ $$\begin{array}{r} 12 \\ -\ 6 \\ \hline \end{array}$$ $$\begin{array}{r} 12¢ \\ -\ 9¢ \\ \hline \end{array}$$ $$\begin{array}{r} 11 \\ -\ 9 \\ \hline \end{array}$$

Solve.   **Workspace**

5. 11 geese are floating on the water.
3 geese fly away.
How many geese are left floating
on the water?

_____ geese

SUBTRACT FACTS AND TENS

Subtract.

Use ⬜ if you want to.

1. $6 - 4 = \underline{2}$ $7 - 2 = \underline{\quad}$
    $60 - 40 = \underline{20}$ $70 - 20 = \underline{\quad}$

2. $4 - 3 = \underline{\quad}$ $5 - 1 = \underline{\quad}$
    $40 - 30 = \underline{\quad}$ $50 - 10 = \underline{\quad}$

3. $6 - 3 = \underline{\quad}$ $9 - 3 = \underline{\quad}$
    $60 - 30 = \underline{\quad}$ $90 - 30 = \underline{\quad}$

4. $60 - 3 = \underline{\quad}$ $17 - 2 = \underline{\quad}$

5. $32 - 2 = \underline{\quad}$ $53 - 1 = \underline{\quad}$

6. $26 - 2 = \underline{\quad}$ $57 - 3 = \underline{\quad}$

7. $36 - 2 = \underline{\quad}$ $67 - 1 = \underline{\quad}$

8. $79 - 1 = \underline{\quad}$ $27 - 3 = \underline{\quad}$

9. $64 - 3 = \underline{\quad}$ $37 - 2 = \underline{\quad}$

COUNT BACK BY TENS

Count back by tens to subtract.

Use ☐ or ▦ if you want to.

1. $55 - 30 = \underline{25}$

2. $38 - 20 = \underline{\hspace{1cm}}$

3. $47 - 10 = \underline{\hspace{1cm}}$

4. $81 - 30 = \underline{\hspace{1cm}}$

5. $51 - 20 = \underline{\hspace{1cm}}$

6. $65 - 10 = \underline{\hspace{1cm}}$

7. $62 - 30 = \underline{\hspace{1cm}}$

8. $58 - 20 = \underline{\hspace{1cm}}$

9. $43 - 10 = \underline{\hspace{1cm}}$

10. $54 - 30 = \underline{\hspace{1cm}}$

11. $33 - 20 = \underline{\hspace{1cm}}$

12. $41 - 20 = \underline{\hspace{1cm}}$

13. $61 - 30 = \underline{\hspace{1cm}}$

14. $56 - 20 = \underline{\hspace{1cm}}$

15. $85 - 30 = \underline{\hspace{1cm}}$

16. $24 - 10 = \underline{\hspace{1cm}}$

17. $53 - 20 = \underline{\hspace{1cm}}$

18. $37 - 10 = \underline{\hspace{1cm}}$

19. $69 - 30 = \underline{\hspace{1cm}}$

20. $76 - 20 = \underline{\hspace{1cm}}$

21. $48 - 10 = \underline{\hspace{1cm}}$

22. $89 - 30 = \underline{\hspace{1cm}}$

2-DIGIT SUBTRACTION

Subtract.

Use ▭▭▭ or ▱
if you want to.

1. $27 - 4 = \underline{23}$ 2. $36 - 3 = \underline{}$

3. $18 - 7 = \underline{}$ 4. $25 - 6 = \underline{}$

5. $32 - 2 = \underline{}$ 6. $20 - 3 = \underline{}$

7. $15 - 5 = \underline{}$ 8. $37 - 7 = \underline{}$

Solve.   **Workspace**

9. 34 people are playing in the band.
7 of them stop playing.
How many people are playing
in the band now?

$34 - 7 = 27$

_____ people

10. There are 20 bands on the field.
4 bands march away.
How many bands are on the
field now?

_____ bands

11. Show how you subtract $25 - 3$.
Write or draw.

Name: _____

MORE SUBTRACTION

Subtract. Use models to help.

1. 36 − 12 = **24**

2. 42 − 15 = _____

3. 26 − 15 = _____

4. 38 − 18 = _____

5. 33 − 19 = _____

6. 28 − 24 = _____

7. 48 − 13 = _____

8. 24 − 16 = _____

9. 35 − 14 = _____

10. 43 − 15 = _____

11. 18 − 12 = _____

12. 29 − 17 = _____

13. 34 − 16 = _____

14. 46 − 23 = _____

15. 21 − 12 = _____

16. 39 − 14 = _____

17. 44 − 24 = _____

18. 27 − 11 = _____

19. 19 − 13 = _____

20. 49 − 18 = _____

21. 41 − 22 = _____

22. 45 − 23 = _____

23. 32 − 23 = _____

24. 47 − 21 = _____

PROBLEM SOLVING: CHOOSE THE METHOD

Solve. Choose the best method for you.

1. 23 people came to hear the school band. Then 14 more came. How many people came in all?

   Workspace

   _37_ people $23 + 14 = 37$

2. 34 first-grade children are in the band. 12 of them play the drums. How many children do not play the drums?

   _____ children

3. The band had 18 wooden blocks. It got 18 more wooden blocks. How many wooden blocks does the band have now?

   _____ wooden blocks

4. The band has 27 maracas. It has 14 triangles. How many more maracas than triangles does the band have?

   _____ more maracas

Is this
Sonic
Mman?